A HALF OF PATRIOTISM

MEMOIRS OF AN (UNKNOWN) ENGINEER

P. MANIVANNAN

GURU CHARANAM

Dedicated to

All those Government servants who dedicated their lives & career for Nation Building but have gone unnoticed, and have not thought of writing their experiences, thinking that it may not be worth sharing.

Contents

Overview

This book may be a first of its kind written by an unknown engineer and may be a surprise in the hands of the reader, but surely it will give an impact after going through the contents. It narrates the thirty five years of experience of a project engineer/manager and (short term) scientist in offshore engineering services and ocean research. Hope it will motivate many readers to write and record their individual experiences for future reference, taking this as a precedent.

When you go through the contents you will observe that this is neither an autobiography nor a technical or management guide, from the way it is written with more emphasize on bringing out the contribution and support of his colleagues and seniors whom he admired and it is really a tribute/commendation to all such associates.

This will serve as a guide for proper strategy and importance of it, in offshore oil field developments and research projects. Application of innovative techniques and managerial strategy in cost reduction of commercial projects is emphasized. A strong opinion against handing over of national wealth to foreign MNC's for exploitation is explained with example and policy makers may review the strategy presently followed. This book also advocates Ocean Thermal Energy as future source of renewable energy, more specifically for India.

The book will surely motivate engineers, scientists and young readers to dedicate their service to nation building with integrity.

Preface

This small book is intended to leave a small footprint by a humble Government Servant who was preached honesty, integrity, and patriotism from his childhood by his agriculturist father, and this is neither an autobiography nor a technical book. Every human being born in this world leaves a footprint and virtues to follow, but most of them go unnoticed or may be noticed only by a few of their close associates for a while and later no trace of their existence remains to be noted. But only a few recorded experiences in the form of a document made available, help in appreciating such a life as an example to follow. Only on this basis, the book is written as I cannot project any great achievements or show any great path to follow. This contains only part of the experience records which came to my mind from ready memory. It may be possible to add more content and experience details in the next edition as some old diaries and related memories are yet to be searched out.

The motivators to write this book are my wife, Mrs. Sheela Manivannan and my wife's eldest sister's husband, Prof. Tha. Pazhamalai, a renowned Tamil Poet and writer. With their support and strength and with the notion that you need not reach the top, to be eligible to share good values and the satisfaction you derive from following such values.

I decided to write this book in English as it contains more of technical content which I am not capable of writing in Tamil for easy understanding of everyone.

The title "A HALF OF PATRIOTISM" was chosen because of two great friends, one who studied with me in Engineering College and another who was a Colleague in ONGC. They are.

1) Shri. R. Chidambaram - (Rasi among friends)
2) Shri. MRN Swamy

In my college autograph Rasi(R. Chidambaram) wrote

"Dear Pondy, (I hail from a village called Vinayagapuram near Pondicherry)

Have a full of joys,

A half of patriotism,

A quarter of humanism…." It goes like this and ends with his best wishes.

On the day of retirement from Oil and Natural Gas Corporation (ONGC), Shri.MRN, Swamy, a senior officer in ONGC, presented a write up "Thank you Mr. Manivannan, ONGCian of rare intelligence and exceptional integrity" and concluded the writing "It is not the absence of opportunities which made Mr. Manivannan to continue in ONGC, in spite of his best-in-class credentials in the field; it was his whole hearted commitment to National Energy Security that made him to continue and retire from ONGC, notwithstanding his slow professional growth. This makes me remember an adage; "Do not worry if you are not successful as successful people enrich themselves from the society than enriching the society".

I am thankful to my parent organization ONGC for grooming me to build up my expertise. I am equally thankful to National Institute of Ocean Technology(NIOT) and Ministry of Earth Sciences (MOES) for giving me senior advisory positions on the basis of my expertise, notwithstanding my position in ONGC, to serve the country.

I hope the readers from the engineering/scientist community will benefit from the experiences I have shared. Though it is only a small part of my experiences and whatever comes to my memory readily, with some papers, records readily available to share and not exhaustive, may be later I can add more in future if welcomed by readers. Hopefully, it will be good reading material to motivate young minds to serve the country without expecting much in return in terms of positions and status.

My acceptance speech on retirement concluded thanking Mr. MRN Swamy for the writeup on me and with my saying "I feel proud that I have given more and taken less."

I would like to quote few lines from the book "Leading from the Front" written by Dr. Col.S.P.Wahi, former CMD, ONGC.

"There has been quite a few top level professional managers who in their passion and loyalty for their profession and more importantly in a gallant spirit of patriotism for their new and resurgent country have performed for their PSEs, in virtual defiance of the bureaucracy and not infrequently at great risk to their personal careers"

Once again, I would like to say that this type of write up may encourage middle level contributors to share their experiences and motivate many countrymen to serve the country with gratitude and without expectations. In my opinion, those who are stubborn and practice honesty and integrity as principles, do not lose balance even when opportunity, circumstances and need drive them otherwise. Hence, I dedicate this book to all such unnoticed Patriotic minds.

JAIHIND!

Acknowledgements

My acknowledgements and thanks are due to all my colleagues and co-workers both senior and junior with whose co-ordinated efforts and support, helped in the little contribution I could make towards energy security and nation building.

Many thanks to the scientists and engineers who inspired me to think of innovation and economization of ocean structures and strategies towards commercial sense.

My sincere thanks to Mr. M. Thyagaraj, Executive Director (Retd), ONGC and Prof. Dr. M.Ravindran, Founder Director, NIOT, for their(foreword/review) for this small book, with their blessings.

My thanks are also due to Dr. P.Rajagopal, CGM(Retd), ONGC, Dr. Raju Abraham, Scientist-G, NIOT, Mr. J.Vijayakumar, CGM(Retd), ONGC and Mr. G.Nallappan, GM(Retd), ONGC for their review and views on the book.

Needless to say my thanks to Prof. Tha.Pazhamalai, who inspired me to write this book and also with his "Aninthurai" in Tamil.

I have taken guidance from Dr. S. Sivasanker (my brother-in-law), former scientist, NCL, Pune (CSIR Laboratory) and Chair-Prof. IIT, Madras for shaping the book, and writing a foreword for this book. He is a renowned scientist in India with more than 200 publications and a guide to many national/international students for their Phd thesis work and his blessings for this write-up is acknowledged. The affection and support of my wife Mrs. Sheela Manivannan was a great strength and help throughout my career. Her sacrifice to cut-short her prestigious career to take care of family and my aspirations to excel in my chosen field is remembered.

Thanks are also due to my brother-in-law Shri. R.Srinivasan M.A., B.L., (my wife's youngest brother) who supported my family to enable me to devote maximum time for office duty and also during my outstation movements.

My sons, Kalyan Sunder Manivannan and Shyam Sunder Manivannan who suggested to add some drawings and photos relevant to a few technical descriptions, the cover page and also few drawings from my rough sketch to final shape are of value addition to the book.

Our family is grateful to Dr. Mrs. Ananthakrishna, MBBS. MD., DCH renowned Peadiatrician and retired Professor, and her late husband Major. P.S. Moorthy for providing health care as well as guiding us spritually all throughout our life and shaping our children with ethics and value which gives us great satisfaction and also immense strength in all our testing times.

Thanks are due to M/S Sree Lingam Printers, Mylapore, Chennai - 600 004 for extending their help in typing. My thanks are due to Mr. Allan and Mrs. Sheila D'Souza for making necessary corrections, Mr. P. Anandhan for compiling the photos and inputs and Notion Press, for publishing the book as desired.

பேராசிரியர். த. பழமலய்

விழுப்புரம்

அணிந்துரை

திரு. ப. மணிவண்ணன், தேசப்பற்று மிக்க ஒரு பொறியாளர். விழுப்புரம் மாவட்டம், விநாயகபுரம் ஒரு சிற்றூர். இவ்வூரில் ஓர் எளிய விவசாயக் குடும்பத்தைச் சேர்ந்த தெரு கூத்து கலைஞர் திரு. ஷி.ழி. பரசுராமக் கவுண்டர் - விஜயலட்சுமி இணையருக்குத் தலை மகனாகப் பிறந்தவர் திரு. ப. மணிவண்ணன்.

இவர் பிறந்த நாள் 12.05.1957 (பதிவு. 12.03.1957) இவருடன் பிறந்தவர்கள் ப.கமலக் கண்ணன், ப. பஞ்சவர்ணம் (தங்கை) ப. கருணாகரன் ஆகியோர். நல்ல நிலையில் உள்ளனர்.

இவர் அய்ந்தாவது வரை விநாயகபுரத்திலும், 6-8 சேமங்கலத்திலும், 9-11 திருச்சிற்றம்பலம் கூட்டுச் சாலை காந்தி உயர்நிலைப்பள்ளியிலும், புகுமுக வகுப்பு (அ. பிரிவு), 1973-74 இல், கடலூர் அரசுக் கலைக் கல்லூரியிலும், பொறியியல் (எந்திரவியல்) 1974 - 79இல், சேலம் அரசுப் பொறியியல் கல்லூரியிலும் பயின்றவர்.

இவருடைய தந்தையார் தேசப்பற்று மிக்கவர், இதனாலேயே மணிவண்ணனும் மண்ணின் மைந்தராய் இம்மண்ணின் முன்னேற்றத்தைக் கருத்தில் கொண்டு, வெளிநாட்டுப் பணிகளில் ஆர்வம் இல்லாதவராய் உள்நாட்டுப் பணியில் சேர்ந்தார். 1980-82 இல் முது தொழில்நுட்பமும் முடித்தார்.

திரு. ப. மணிவண்ணன், தம் பள்ளி ஆண்டுகளில் வகுப்பில் முதல் மாணவராகத் தேறியவர். பின்னை ஆண்டுகளிலும், பொருளாதார நெருக்கடிகளால் (நாள், வார, மாத, ஏன் ஆண்டு வருமான உறுதி இல்லாத

குடும்பங்கள் தாமே விவசாயக் குடும்பங்கள்) சிரமப்பட்டு படித்தாலும் தன் தகுதிகளைத் தக்க வைத்துக்கொண்டவர்.

வெளி உலக விவகாரங்களிலும் விளையாட்டுகளிலும் ஆர்வம் காட்டாத மணிவண்ணன், இலக்கிய உணர்வு உடையவராய் கவிதைகள், கதைகள் எழுதி வந்திருக்கிறார். பிறகு, பணிக்காலத்தில், துறை சார்ந்த சாதனைகளிலேயே ஈடுபாடு கொண்டவராய், பல கருத்தரங்குகளில் கலந்து கொண்டு ஆய்வுக் கட்டுரைகள் வழங்கியுள்ளார்.

மணிவண்ணன் அவர்கள் கடல்சார்ந்த பணிகள் புரிந்தவர். பாரதக் கடலின் பல பகுதிகளிலும் திட்டங்கள் பலவற்றிலும் பங்குப் பணியாற்றியவர். இவருடைய பழகும் பண்புக்காகவும், புதிய புதிய ஆலோசனைகளுக்காகவும், இவருடன் பணியாற்றியவர்களால் இவர் மிகவும் மதிக்கப்பட்டவர். 1982-2017 ஆண்டுகளில் துறையினரால் மெச்சத் தகுந்த பணியாற்றிப் பணி ஓய்வு பெற்றுள்ள மணிவண்ணன் நேற்றைப் போலவும் இன்றும் நாளையும் தேசப்பற்று மிக்க ஒரு திறமையான பொறியாளர்.

இவருடையதுணைவியார்ரெ.ஷீலா,மனையியல்எம்.எஸ்.சி.,எம்.பில்., எம்.எட்., படித்தவர். புதுச்சேரி சமூக நலத்துறையிலும், சென்னை அப்பலோ மருத்துவ மனையிலும் சில காலம் பணியாற்றி விலகிக் கொண்டவர். கணவர் உடல் நலனிலும், பிள்ளைகள் கல்வி முன்னேற்றத்திலும் அக்கறைதான் காரணம்! நியாந்தானே! இவர்கள் மக்கள் கல்யாண் சுந்தர், ஷ்யாம் சுந்தர் பொறியியல் பட்டதாரிகளாய் அமெரிக்காவில் வேலைகளில் உள்ளனர். எதிர்காலத்திய இளைஞர்களின் ஊக்கத்திற்கும் உயர்விற்கும் இந்நூல், ஓர் ஊந்து விசையாய், வழிகாட்டியாய் இருந்து வரும். திரு. மணிவண்ணன் அவர்கள் குடும்பத்தினருக்கும், நண்பர்களுக்கும் இந்திய மக்கள் சார்பாய் நம்முடைய பாராட்டுதல்களும் வாழ்த்துகளும் என்றைக்கும் உரியன. வாழ்க!

பேராசிரியர். த. பழமலய்

விழுப்புரம்

9942646942

14.11.2023

M. THYAGARAJ
Executive Director, ONGC (Retd)
Chairman, PETRO DIGITAL PVT LTD,
Chennai, Tamil Nadu

Foreword

I read this book titled "A Half of Patriotism"- written by Mr. P Manivannan dedicated to all those Government servants who dedicated their life & career for Nation Building but gone unnoticed, and not thought of writing their experiences…. The author's agony for sharing one's valuable life time experiences is right and respectable. Because Govt invests heavily on human power and development on their payroll for the growth of the country and not merely providing employment. An employee during his service devises many ways and new methods to solve the issues, but the organisation has no means to capture such tacit knowledge. Of late many organisations and the establishments of the Govt owned companies have been creating knowledge management portals. 20 years back superannuated employees would walk away with a heavy mind, full of acquired knowledge to their home, only to switch off. So, we extend our thanks to the author for taking this bold initiative open mindedly.

Shri P Manivannan had been my junior colleague in my team of ONGC, for more than 20 years of service. He hails from a decent family and he is a well-behaved person. I know him well and his abilities. He had been my team leader by possessing various personality traits worth mentioning here the following top Ten: -

1. He is a trust worthy individual, time tested with lots of patience, resilience and consistent in behaviour.
2. He had always oriented himself towards the organisational goals.
3. He quickly understands and judges the situational issues at work and tries to resolve using best and proven methods
4. He was able to gauge the threats in the job and able to convert opportunities out of them.
5. He used new and innovative methods where ever he faced challenges in the work.
6. He is agile and able to adjust himself to new developments in the organisational growth.
7. He scans the new technological developments and able to convert them to derive advantage.
8. He is a good negotiator of contractual terms in major projects, with convincing arguments, to benefit the organisation.
9. He was a good guide, tutor, and mentor to his subordinates, and settled their problems amicably.
10. He possesses excellent traits for a good leadership such as; interpersonal relations, compassion towards subordinates, training and development.

Having said that above, the following are the Top Ten works of his commendable performance where he actually displayed his personality traits in ONGC:

1. He played a key role in the Engineering and Construction of Offshore Oil & Gas field surface facilities like Platforms,

pipelines and plants in the early development of Mumbai offshore fields in the Arabian sea.

2. He was instrumental in solving many issues related to offshore constructional activities surfaced out during offshore installation.

3. He was successful in managing the fabrication and installation at offshore site on behalf of ONGC as Company Representative, day to day supervision and sign off maintaining ONGC's interests.

4. He suggested innovative and cost-effective solutions to the complicated threats during the offshore construction, that could save time and brought economic advantage.

5. He participated in many contractual negotiations during pre-award of the major offshore contracts and successfully resolved a number of issues that arose in the bidding stage.

6. He worked over long stretched hectic days of the projects to avoid the situations to go out of control.

7. He enjoyed the trust of ONGC and earned respect from the contractors during the execution of major projects of ONGC by his impartial and unbiased approach.

8. He was a key player in the project coordination & management in bringing Oil & Gas production from the virgin field known as RAVVA Offshore which established new eastern subcontinent of proven hydrocarbon in the Oil & Gas Map of India.

9. He also experienced many new harsh challenges offered by Eastern offshore in Bay of Bengal during implementation of RAVVA, as compared to relatively less severe conditions at Arabian Sea in the Western offshore. This offered him creative design opportunities against the threats offered by the environmental conditions in the east coast, and he was able to implement various engineering solutions.

10. His above experience in East coast provided him more confidence and comprehension in further exploiting the hunt for Oil & Gas in the deeper waters towards the inter continental shelf of the east coast for implementation of new caisson technology for the field...

His overall exposure and life time experience along with his personal traits in the corporate organisation, provided him a great confidence and a bold step towards this compilation. I am sure that this book will bring out his vast and varied experience, from the suspended animation of so-called retirement to real life useful lessons. Shri P Manivannan has been married to Smt. Sheela, a well-educated teacher, a simple & humble lady, and without her continuous support and cooperation in difficult and hectic situations in his career path, he could not have won accolades. Without her motivation this book could not have come out. They are blessed with two sons, both of them are Engineers, working in the USA.

I wish him great success in his endeavour.

- M. Thyagaraj

Dr. S. Sivasanker
Retd. Scientist-G,
National Chemical Laboratory, Pune
(Also, Ex-Chair Professor,
I.I.T., Madras, Chennai)

Foreword

It is my pleasure to write this foreword to Manivannan's book, "A Half of Patriotism-Memoirs of an Engineer". Manivannan is a mechanical engineer with an M.Tech. degree from the Indian Institute of technology, Madras who worked in ONGC in different locations in India. He also worked in NIOT, Chennai on deputation for a few years.

At ONGC, Manivannan specialized in offshore work pertaining to the erection of platforms for oil exploration and production in Mumbai offshore basin on the West coast and Krishna-Godavari basin on the East coast. The book presents his experiences as an offshore engineer describing the dangers and difficulties of working in the sea, and the pleasures of successful completion of the planned structures. During his stint in Assam (ONGC), he implemented the laying of the Khoraghat to Borolla crude pipeline. The book describes the many innovations of his that led to monetary savings for his employer, ONGC.

During the later stages of his career, Manivannan joined NIOT on deputation for 3 years. During this period, he worked on the design and testing of offshore plants (OTEC) for energy production using the temperature gradient that exists between the water on the surface of the ocean and its depth. The advantage of OTEC plants is that they can produce electricity 24 hours a day throughout the year compared to the seasonal nature of wind turbines and sunlight based solar power generation.

In the book, Manivannan gratefully points out that he was lucky to have received guidance and support from seniors from ONGC and NIOT where he worked and from collaborating organizations and contractors like EIL, HSL and MDL.

The title of the book, "A Half of Patriotism…" expresses the author's patriotic feelings, inculcated into him by his father, that drove him to work in India and contribute to its growth, un-enamored by more lucrative employment opportunities outside India.

I believe that this book will be highly inspirational to engineers and educative to lay men, who can learn about the nuances of offshore oil production.

It is pertinent to note that he has achieved so much as a specialist engineer despite his rural background, being born to minimally educated parents with modest means. Therefore, this book should also be inspirational to youngsters from rural areas and economically backward sections.

Manivannan is my brother-in-law married to my youngest sister Sheela. Sheela has been an immense support to her husband throughout his professional career, forsaking her own career as a nutritionist. She has proved the adage "behind every successful man, there is a woman".

I congratulate Manivannan for this well written book and wish him success in publishing it.

- Dr. S. Sivasanker

Prof. Dr. M. Ravindran
Founder Director of NIOT
Chennai.

Review Comments

I am very happy to write these review comments on the book titled "A HALF OF PATRIOTISM-Memoirs of an unknown Engineer" written by Mr. Manivannan. He served in NIOT during 2001 to 2004.

He came on deputation from ONGC.

NIOT was started in 1993 when there were not many senior engineers with offshore experience. So the contributions of Mr. Manivannan during his service was very valuable. He worked mainly in the development of technology and demonstration activities for the installation of 1 MW OTEC plant off-Tuticorin and in the desalination plant in Kavaratti, Lakshadweep for generation of drinking water as a by-product.

Mr. Manivannan also co-authored in 2004/2005, a techno commercial report on the establishment of an OTEC plant in India. I believe a commercial OTEC plant will be installed in India soon, in view of its merits for tropical regions.

Mr. Manivannan is among the senior scientists of ONGC/ NIOT, who planned the development of offshore R&D work. I am very glad that Mr. Manivannan has written this book containing his experience in offshore works in India.

I am very sure that this book will be of immense importance and use for offshore research in India. I wish him all success with his new book.

- Prof. Dr. M. Ravindran

P. Rajagopal
GM(P)-Ret.

Review Comments

A HALF OF PATRIOTISM – Book review

Mr. Manivannan the author of this book, "A HALF OF PATRIOTISM-Memoirs of an Engineer", is a competent Mechanical Engineer graduated from a reputed institute in India, joined ONGC at a tender age and moulded himself in works related to oil and gas environment. He gained vast experience of over 30 years in engineering and construction field both offshore and onshore structures and equipment design, fabrication, installation, and commissioning. His contribution as construction engineer can be cited while Heera ph-I platform fabrication, load out, and installation by MDL. He has achieved many cost reductions during the implementation of construction works like making temporary flow line for early commissioning of Heera process complex. At times when work demanded, he used to stay long days offshore without a break and even losing personal financial gains to complete the work. It is interesting to note that his proactive action avoided standby time of barge which saved rig time and thereby a financial gain to ONGC during jacket installation. On a personal front, his quick and appropriate action at the worksite saved a welder from drowning in the sea and also saved a quality control engineer from an accident. He was also involved in design review at NSC fabrication yard for HD/HE well platform wherein with the technical support of EIL team he could overcome the pressure of the contractor to take deviation on material specification.

The author was instrumental in designing a new equipment layout to accommodate a crane to operate 360 deg instead of 270 deg which was implemented in HD/HE well platform. He could incorporate 9 well slots instead of 6 wells. This cost saving innovation was appreciated by ONGC management. However, the same management removed him from a high value project having foreign chances. He has also brought in innovations in loading out jackets without sump caissons but providing only clamps to facilitate installation at site at a future date. Also, he made innovation with a new construction technique for mud mat weight reduction of offshore platforms which was patented by ONGC. Burial of offshore pipeline improves stability. He could implement self-burial technique for GS-15/23 offshore marginal field development.

His capability of taking quick decisions is revealed in the techno commercial meeting of Ravva phase 2. Even though with hardship Ravva phase-1 was developed and excellent oil production achieved, but transferring the total asset to private parties at this stage could not be avoided as it was policy matters. Development of Ravva Phase-2 is another challenge where in, the author was involved in technical review and recommended a bridge connecting RA and RC platforms instead of constructing another platform one Km away which saved the cost involved in laying a pipeline and helideck.

The author briefly explained his association with development of PY-3, an offshore project, in the hands of JV and its failure in implementation and revenue generation. The author observed that his proposal of subsea wells and flowline, construction of a well platform at shallow depth and crude processing at landfall point, transportation of crude to Refinery and natural gas to GAIL would prolong PY-3 for longer years and generate more revenue by utilizing the natural gas also, comparing to the operator's proposal of subsea completion, deployment of FPSO, producing only oil and burning natural gas. However, with out giving weightage to the author's suggestions, the operator went ahead with implementation of their proposal and ultimately landed in an early closure of operation due to uneconomical reason.

Another innovative implementation the author was involved in was the construction of the world's smallest platform GS-15-4, which weighed only 320 tons. In addition, there were many cost reduction measures, chiefly a monopole design for GS-15-4 and GS-23-1. The author was proud that these platforms and related pipelines served for their design life and even sustain Tsunami. He was awarded by, Chairman ONGC for his contribution in many challenges in facilities construction and cost savings to ONGC. Any marginal field is to be developed in a phased manner by knowing the success at each stage. One such field is GS-15/G1, where it was initially planned for modular concept. But however, as claimed by the author, later it was executed by integrating as a mega project at a huge initial investment and landed into failure due to very poor return on investment.

GS-15/G1 and PY-3 developments are examples, the author suggested that heavy loss was due to improper planning and could have happened due to transfers of experienced officers who handled the projects. These are some areas where Transfer policy needs attention by looking into the possibility of retaining experienced persons at least till the completion of such key projects.

The author on deputation to NIOT contributed to OTEC projects towards conversion of ocean thermal energy to electricity. Even after his deputation to NIOT his services were required in ONGC for positioning of drilling rig over well GS-15/23 for its drilling and its completion proved his technical competency. Though this concept of well platform was conceived and completed with the effort of the author he could not enjoy the fruit of commissioning as at that juncture the project was transferred to some other group. The author listed many other similar misfortunes wherein he was actively involved but could not reap the fruit of commissioning and celebrations. On deputation to NIOT, the author was heading OTEC project for extraction of offshore thermal energy and Desalination plant to supply fresh water. Based on the success of pilot desalination plant at Kavaratti, 6 more numbers of LTTD plants were built for the benefit of other Islands. He also presented few papers for the national and international level conferences. He also worked for offshore wind energy.

On completion of the deputation period, the author was placed at Assam (Jorhat) wherein he worked for on-shore engineering services. While serving at Assam he encountered many challenges in implementation of Khoraght-Barola trunk pipeline right from tendering and awarding and execution. In addition, the author contributed his technical competency to solving soil analysis and metering facilities of associated gas for supply to GAIL and repair of the approach road to ONGC site. The author also brought out the risk involved and thrilling experience while travel from Jorhat to Khoragat due to threat of elephants sighted on road in Nambar forest.

The author tried to backtrack his experiences in his 30 years of service and lessons learnt to the benefit of young readers who are freshly joining engineering and construction jobs in ONGC or elsewhere. Sustainability of freshers in organization such as ONGC, depends on self-esteem and organizational behavior. Before the eighties the employees were more experienced but less educated whereas, beyond the eighties the employees were more educated and had high expectation and less patience. The need of mentoring is pointed out by the author particularly for freshers with higher degrees (MTech/PhDs) entering the organization at induction level to satisfy this imbalance. Overall the book is worth reading and useful for freshers. My hearty congratulations to both the author and reader of this book.

- P. Rajagopal

J.Vijayakumar
Retired Chief General Manager(Finance&Accounts)
& Regional Audit Head of Southern Region, ONGC
Chennai.

Review

It is a great pleasure to write my review comments on the book titled "A HALF OF PATRIOTISM-Memoirs of an unknown Engineer" written by Shri.P.Manivannan, being one of the stalwarts of the 1982 GT Batches of ONGC.

1982 GT Batches of all disciplines contributed positions to ONGC internally from Chairman Cum Managing Director, Directors, Executive Directors, Group General Managers, Chief General Managers, General Managers and Deputy General Managers. From the above positions, every GT of 1982 would be pleased to see the above book as their own due to ONGC's HR Policy and treatment given by Top Management/Central Government to every ONGC 1982 GT Trainee.

Being GT Batch from Finance, I have seen Shri.Manivannan's contributions closely after his joining in Chennai. His contributions are vividly explained in his book and some are not utilised by ONGC and hence a great National Loss. During my Ravva Joint Venture audit, technical team of the Operator, Cairn Energy India would tell about the design of Shri.Manivannan with economical structures and flow lines and appreciated by foreign consultants on its intricacies.

Similarly in Hardy Oil Exploration Joint Venture Audit, we had observed that flow line from the offshore well near Puducherry to Nagapattinam Refinery would have evacuated last drop/quantity of oil/Gas as compared to floating oil tanker production, hired by the PY3 Joint Venture which led to premature closure of its operation resulting in Great National Loss.

I am very sure that this book will be a great lesson to all Engineering and Management Trainees in India with respect to proper strategy while planning. I wish him all success with his new book.

- J. Vijayakumar

राष्ट्रीय समुद्र प्रौद्योगिकी संस्थान
वेलच्चेरी – तांबरम रोड, नारायणपुरम, पल्लिकरणै, चेन्नै – 600 100, भारत.
National Institute of Ocean Technology
Velachery - Tambaram Road, Narayanapuram, Pallikaranai, Chennai - 600 100 INDIA.
फोन / Phone : 044 66783300 , फैक्स / Fax : 044 22460275 GSTIN# 33AAATNO530G1Z6
वेबसाइट / Website : www.niot.res.in, ISO 9001 Certified Institution

Dr. Raju Abraham
Scientist-G
National Institute of Ocean Technology
Velachery-Tambaram Main Road
Chennai 600 100

Review Comments

I am delighted to have read the autobiographical book titled 'A Half of Patriotism-memoirs of an unknown engineer' by P. Manivannan, which covers his extensive experience in ocean research and related activities. The book provides a profound understanding of ocean-related problems and challenges he had faced. Manivannan has dedicated many years of service to ONGC and was also deputed to the Ocean Thermal Energy Conversion (OTEC) project at NIOT. Both ONGC and NIOT have significantly contributed to harnessing energy from the sea, one in the non-renewable form and the other in the renewable form. Due to the efforts for reducing carbon emissions, renewable energy is gaining prominence throughout the world and his contributions will be a land mark for the future.

I had the privilege of working under P. Manivannan during his four-year deputation to NIOT. He was a soft-spoken yet astute engineer. On several occasions, we sailed together and resided on floating platforms in the vast ocean exchanging ideas and dreams. Our work primarily revolved around shallow and deep water tests related to OTEC. Manivannan played an active role in the assembly, integration, and deployment of the deep-sea mooring system, a challenging and risky aspect of the project. His straightforward, yet highly practical approach to complex problems left a lasting impression on my mind. His unique perspectives on the social and economic aspects of OTEC were immensely valuable to the scientific community at NIOT during that time. He has significantly contributed for the R&D activities of NIOT on renewable energy and desalination in addition to the offshore related project activities. He had strong views on independent mooring system for the OTEC barge which later proved to be practical and successful. We have together prepared a comprehensive techno-commercial report Feasibility Study for Setting up Ocean Thermal Energy Conversion (OTEC) Based Power Projects in India for NTPC in 2005. I do hope that these site specific studies will be a guide for the future OTEC activities in India.

Manivannan was not only compassionate but also considerate and approachable to all his colleagues and subordinates. These qualities in him developed deep bonds among us. I am grateful to God and his family for his fruitful contributions and wish him continued success in the future.

- Dr. Raju Abraham

AZHAGU TAMIL DESIYAM (ATD)

"We Can't say that what could not be done in the past cannot be done in future as well" - Nallappanar. G

G. Nallappan	K. Valarmathi	S. Parandhaman
Founder - President	General Secretary	Treasurer

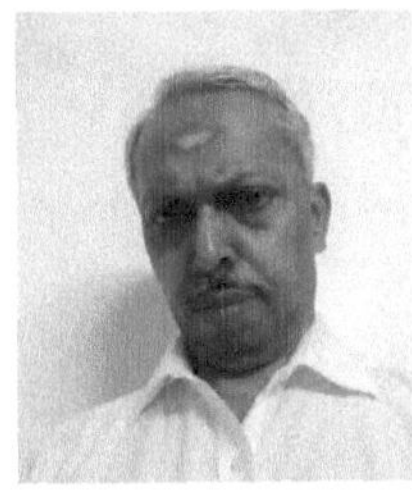

G.Nallappan
President, ATD
General Manager
Rtd. From ONGC

Review Comments

This book titled ""A half of patriotism-memoirs of an Unknown Engineer" running in to 150 pages contains the real life journey of one of the top talents (Mr. Manivannan) born in our country in a nondescript village called Vinayagapuram in Pondicherry.

Here I must say how I got attracted towards him: The bond between himself and me started sometime in 2010 when I found him to possess the following important human qualities

1. Honest and hence not fearing anyone
2. Simple looking & truth speaking

3. Not hurting others for anything
4. Kind & humble approach towards all humans
5. Intelligent, eloquent and impressive in speeches
6. Capable of differentiating between what is good & what is bad
7. Encouraging good humans while keeping away from bad ones
8. Never hankering after money, power, prestige, fame etc.,
9. Always remains impartial, unbiased and fair-minded

These qualities made me get closer to him very fast and that is being sustained even today and I hope that will continue forever.

Mr. Manivannan's knowledge and experience are so vast and rich that one could count him to be one of top technocrats in the country. I being a human resource planner-cum-management expert, always sought his help and advice in understanding technical issues to solve complex management issues to earn profits for the organization as every wrong management decision would lead to losing profits or displeasing the workers. I was also taking his advice on student projects meant to expose the final year students who had to work on practical problem to enhance their skills, just before completion of their degree courses. He is not only a technocrat but also a motivator of humans to do things better, if they - are doing something and if they do nothing, he can make them do something instead of wiling away their time. As such, he is an excellent human being.

Very recently also, I sought his advice on how to generate income for the government as and when total prohibition is implemented, as the successive governments are not ready to implement the same and the excuse they all give is that alcohol sales in the state gives them substantial revenue to run the government and hence the need to continue with it. Here, Mr. Manivannan very convincingly gave a suggestion that the distilleries which produce variety of drinks can be easily converted/modified into ETHANOL producing plants using almost the same ingredients such as molasses, high-starch plants, grains, berries & yeast. Infact, he came out with a total solution to the problem of revenue deficit in the state by saying that ETHANOL can be used as a fuel in automobiles by mixing it with petrol and that sale revenue will be quite substantial and he also added that if all the mineral resources like sand, granite, graphite etc are brought under the control of government then there will be enough revenue to run the state and therewith the revenue deficit will vanish for ever. This is how his brain works to solve every problem, both technical and non-technical.

Myself, being a HR person used to witness frequent transfers of personnel which means disturbance from place to place and job to job and in this context, I had an argument with Mr. Manivannan and he was of the opinion that frequent job rotation will go against building expertise in a person and hence our HR policies should be reviewed and modified and as he rightly said, this became a point of discussion and consideration from one-in-5 year job rotation to one in 10-year-relation and that became the guideline for all transfers in future. The reason for mentioning this is that being a technical person, he could think deeply about the human aspects as well, which is what is required of a good leader and he excelled in that too.

By writing this book, Mr. Manivannan ji has certainly brought out the strenuous efforts of all hard working technocrats not only in ONGC, but also others doing similar roles in harnessing the energy and other natural resources across the country. This book illustrates the importance and the sense of responsibility they hold towards securing our country's Oil & Gas production and other vital resources, thereby securing the nation's and the citizen's future. I am sure it must have been his rare intelligence and upright qualities that must have driven him to write down his work experiences which can surely be an eye opener to many in the country.

Finally, I wish him a very long life to serve the people and the country with utmost devotion!

- G.Nallappan

Chapter 1

Joining ONGC at Dehradun

I joined ONGC at KDMIPE, Dehradun (a town in Uttar Pradesh state of India), which is the Head quarters for ONGC, on 01.07.1982 as AEE(Mech) and got the training for three months and later posted to Bombay.

The training covered various stages of oil exploration and production and class room lectures on various topics like survey, geology, paleontology, drilling, production technology, reservoir engineering, construction and maintenance of equipment and facilities, finance and HR policies. It was good and very interesting to know the nuances of an E&P company. Everyone had their own imagination and understanding of the topics and being mechanical engineers, our role was clearly brought out by the faculty in various areas of requirement.

At the outset, I had visualized that probably with my higher education in Tribology, it would be appropriate to serve in the area of condition monitoring and preventive maintenance of large turbines and various equipment on drilling rigs and production installations.

Only when I was posted to Bombay, it took a different turn that I had to become an engineer, and a scientist on offshore engineering services and ocean technologies with little exposure to quality assurance and onshore engineering services.

* * *

Chapter 2

Bombay E & C Division

I shifted to Mumbai offshore project from Oct'82.

On joining, Shri.K.Anjaneyan sir, GM (C) asked me whether I wanted to join E & C or E & P. One was a construction group dealing with project implementation at field, and the other dealt with planning of field developments. I preferred E & C as suggested by some friends, especially senior Tamil friends in ONGC.

From1982 Oct to 1991 May, I served at E & C division, Mumbai.

My first Helicopter ride to an offshore site was in Oct 1982 for assisting the ONGC representative on DB-14, Mc Dermott barge, undertaking Installation and Commissioning of QST well platforms in Bombay High, South. Sri.D.Sharan, AEE(P) also accompanied me for getting trained in offshore activities.

While on this assignment, I learnt to communicate by Radio. I was very thrilled and found it interesting.

I travelled in a boat to move to a platform (unmanned) located on the other side of where the barge was stationed to a different location for pre-commissioning activities. There was quite some difficulty in transferring from boats to barge and barge to boat, as well as from boat to platform & vice versa.

I once escaped from getting crushed in between the gap of a barge & boat while jumping to the barge from the boat. D.Sharan, AEE(P) saved me by holding my hand strongly and lifting me up into the barge. We had to wait on the boat top deck level and quickly jump on to the barge when the levels of the barge and boat-deck nearly matched. As the boat was moving up and down heavily in bad weather, this was a risky activity. During such times personal transfer between boat and barge is generally done by the crawler crane (Manitowec) on the barge by using a personal basket.

I quickly learnt many engineering aspects of the design and installation of offshore platforms by reading the bid-packages, drawings and manuals.

Interaction with Mr. Peter Dixon, field engineer, Mr. Buddy Quinn, Piping engineer of McDermott and EIL inspection engineers (consultants to ONGC) largely helped me in quickly understanding the pre-commissioning activities of piping systems and equipment on the well platforms.

When some EIL inspectors refused to travel by boat in bad weather, I dared to go along with the field engineer by boat to witness the hydrotest of piping systems. This was very challenging, and I enjoyed the adventure besides learning technically gainful jobs. This helped me in learning the systems very fast. The field engineer and piping engineer explained the testing methodology as per codes and genuinely conducted the tests. Though I was new they never bypassed a test or procedure and explained thoroughly and obtained my signature only after I understood and was satisfied with the explanation and procedures and results. The higher qualification I obtained (M.Tech) at IIT Madras earned me respect from the field engineer Peter Dixon who was from MIT, USA. Thus, it was a good start and I gained a good knowledge on the top side of well platforms.

A senior project manager of McDermott spread the information in the base office that I had a good ability to grasp the technical aspects and possessed the right aptitude and approach/ideas to complete the pre-commissioning activities; this information was also shared with my senior bosses at ONGC. This first step progressively made me build up expertise on offshore structures, design aspects, fabrication procedures load out, transportation and installation activities etc.

After 3-4 years of experience, I was branded as an advisor and problem solver in offshore E & C projects controlled by one GM (C). Senior Engineers in EIL also gave the respect and mentioned my abilities to the other consultants to ONGC. I accompanied GM (C) to offshore sites, when he visited the many barges on the same day to resolve technical and interface problems, in peak offshore working season.

Senior people from EIL and offshore experts like Dr. Hariharan, Mr. G.Raman, Shri. Jayaraman, Shri. PMV Subramanian, Shri. Ramalingam, Shri. B. Ghosh are some senior experts whom I respect, and seek their advise. I came to be closely associated with them and was respected for my work. This enabled obligations of mutual conveniences and priorities over projects handled by our team, with the project coordinator Shri. E. Venugopal.

Coming back to my first offshore trip, in Nov'82 a cyclone was announced by IMD in Arabian Sea near Bombay High and the barges were advised to move away from the cyclone area. DB-14 moved towards North to keep a safe distance away from cyclone. Captain Bobby Joe Kelly was in command of the barge. The construction barges are generally made without propulsion system and are towed to various sites by tug boats and maneuvered and anchored with eight anchors on location. Hence DB-14 had to be towed to a safer location.

- Cyclonic conditions started soon. As helicopters could not fly, senior officers who came on a visit to the barge to review the progress also had to stay back on barge DB-14. Shri.C.K.Srinivasan, Chief Engineer ONGC, Shri. Lakshmanan, Sr. Project manager, Mc Dermott, Shri.J.K.Popli, SE(Mech) and a few others were on board to experience the worst cyclone while stuck on the barge.

- It was unfortunate that instead of moving away from the cyclone, we moved into the eye of the cyclone. The holding and tow by tugboats were becoming extremely difficult.

- Equipment like cranes etc., was stowed & secured on the barge deck for safety. During the job, the rigger superintendent got injured and fractured one of his hands. The doctor on-board put bandages on him and treated him. Even movements inside the barge were becoming extremely difficult. The hatch, sealing the barge living quarters was tightly closed.

Due to further severity of cyclone, the towing boat Jaramac-17 could not hold or tow the barge and hence it got disconnected, and the barge was put on storm anchor. The towing tug and another support vessel Vivian-Tide were following at a safe distance away.

Power broke down on the barge. The captain also started feeling the risk of loss of lives on high seas.

Radio communication was made to different agencies, Indian Navy, American Navy. But no one could help. The barge was like a small match box floating in between two large mountains of water. The next moment the barge was almost submerged and only the splashing of water could be seen from the glass window of the  barge. I could see the maximum wave height physically at a 100-year cyclonic condition, what we read in the bid package design criteria. The wave height could easily be 6 to 9 m or so. As the vessel was drifting on storm anchor, dragging, holding, and pitching, heaving uncontrollably, the captain sent an SOS and he also wrote all the names of the occupants of barge in a sealed box and kept it ready for deployment in the sea as he sensed the risk on the barge getting broken into two or hitting another uncontrolled drifting vessel.

The barge was drifting uncontrollably dragging the storm anchor which held for some time and hence the drifting was slower. People on board had no food after breakfast in the morning of the day and almost everyone was praying for life. People could not sit on chairs. So, they were either lying down or sitting on the floor. The vessel drifted to Surat from Bombay High the next day morning and slowly the weather calmed down. The tugboats then could come next to the barge and the barge was towed. An American (Navy?) ship came around the barge and contacted the captain for safety of the people and then left back.

The captain told me that it took 30 years of sea life to witness a cyclone of this nature by him, whereas I was lucky to witness the same within 30days of my sea life and congratulated me for the same. After the nightmare incident of the cyclone, I returned to the base office.

2.1   Heera PH - I

Within a few days of my 1st offshore visit, I got transferred to Heera field development project, a green field development in water depths in the range of around 40m - 60m. The group was headed by Mr. M.N. Madhava, GM (C) and Shri. E. Venugopal was the Project coordinator. Phase-I consisted of well platforms HA to HE (Five) and one process platform HRA with a capacity of 40,000 BOPD. The processed crude was to be pumped to R-12 process platform complex by a 40km long 12" pipeline for export through oil tankers at R-12. I was fully involved in the fabrication of jackets and topside decks at the Mazagaon dock and the installation of the platforms.

The contract for fabrication, installation and commissioning of HA, HB & HC well platforms, process platform HRA, well fluid pipelines HB-HA, HC-HA and trunk pipeline HRA-R12, which were a major part of HeeraPh-I development, was awarded to MDL (Mazagon Docks Limited).

The fabrication of jackets & decks were done at MDL's main yard and also at their Nhava yard. I was visiting both the yards for fabrication supervision. For visiting Nhava we had to start early in the morning, as it used to be a 2 hour journey from Mumbai, Bandra to Nhava via Panvel. EILinspection engineers were posted at both MDL main yard and Nhava yard. I was coordinating with EIL and MDL engineers on the fabrication activities and inspection works. It was very much a learning experience. As MDL was new to the offshore project, they also interacted very closely with EIL engineers as they had some earlier experience in the inspection, supervision of offshore works in foreign yards for previous ONGC offshore projects of Bombay High. This helped all the new engineers to learn the intricacies of offshore fabrication.

The jacket fabrication involved laying of launch track for load out, assembly of jacket legs and spreading the vertical framings, roll-up of the frames by cranes and temporarily supporting them with tubular members, placing conductor guide framings of all levels of jackets and integrate the jacket in space with all the members by erecting them with cranes and welding them in place. One of the long- lead bought out item, the sump caisson was also part of the jacket and was to be fitted into the jacket. The piles to be driven into the jacket legs were fabricated into segments and marked with foot markings.

Day-to-day technical issues in fabrication were discussed amongst MDL, EIL, ONGC and the subcontractor's engineers. Even engineering analysis on fabrication activities like roll-up were discussed and reviewed which were already done by MDL's engineering department. Dr. Jayaraman who was the engineering manager at MDL was guiding the fabrication engineers in the minor engineering calculations.

Similarly, deck fabrication works were done at the yard. Main deck and helideck were separately fabricated. Boat landing, barge bumpers of the jacket were also separately fabricated for load-out to offshore.

Offshore Platform fabrication, loadout, Installation & Pipeline laying

The deck equipment procurement by MDL was delayed mainly because they were imported items and even indigenization efforts could not help, but only contributed to delay. Every equipment imported was through LC payment and all were custom-cleared for arrival at yard. In view of this, the fabrication completion and load out of decks could not be done together for installation at offshore for taking up drilling. This problem was not faced by foreign contractors as they could complete both jackets and decks together. To avoid drilling delay and early commissioning for oil flow, it was decided to fabricate temporary decks for facilitating drilling and after drilling was completed the temporary decks (without any equipment) were removed and regular main deck and helidecks were installed and oil flow was achieved in the next season. This became a common practice with Indian yards fabricating offshore platforms, like MDL(Mazagon Docks), HSL (Hindustan Shipyard) & BSCL (Burn Standard). I had made arrangements/provision even in the temporary decks for certain minimum facilities required for oil flow, temporarily. It was a welcome move by ONGC to encourage Indian yards including L&T(Larsen & Toubro) for taking up offshore project execution towards indigenization. Had it gone in the right track with continued support from all stake holders, India could have become a large player in the offshore industry. Though it was my thinking, it could not be raised into a vision by any power centre to achieve the same.

Further to the experience and expertise gained in well platforms of MDL, as they were taking up HRA process platform for the first time, along with a living quarter much more knowledge could be gained during procurement, fabrication and installation/commissioning of the process complex. The major equipment like HP separator, LP separator, surge tank, Gas turbine generators, Diesel generators, HVAC system, water makers, Instrument gas systems, lifeboat, etc., were procured, installed and commissioned.

The first platform HA installation and most of the other platforms and their components including commissioning was supervised by me. It was during this time, much experience was gained and expertise on offshore platforms installation could be acquired. Mr. E.Venugopal and Mr. S.R.Trivedi, Mr. M.N.Madhava and few other senior officers guided and imparted their knowledge and also by going through design documents, expertise could be built-up by practically correlating the implementation of events and activities. Dr. Hariharan from (EIL) Engineers India Ltd who was a stalwart in offshore structures engineering gave his valuable guidance and taught nuances of offshore design and some thumb rule guidelines for decision making in offshore works, when sudden technical issues cropped up at offshore.

2.2   Challenges in Heera Ph-I

Some of the challenges faced in the Heera Phase-I are worth mentioning. One of the challenges was to pre-commission the process platform HRA and keep it ready for oil production. Unfortunately, as the process platform deck was loaded out from the yard in a pre-mature state due to a management decision to show the load out completion as per commitment to ONGC by MDL, the hook-up work on the decks was taking longer time in offshore, due to left over works at yard.

It is pertinent to mention that the Mazagaon Docks had for the first time acquired a construction barge in India and this was also used in the execution

of Heera works. The name of the barge was Mahavir. I was the first ONGC representative to arrive on Mahavir and start the offshore construction in Heera field after acquisition of this barge by MDL. I was also associated with the crane load-test and various tests on Mahavir barge at Nhava yard, as ONGC representative along with Bureau Veritas, the certification agency surveyor. The offshore operations of MDL were headed by Capt. Shushil Kumar (later he became the Naval chief-Admiral Shushil Kumar) who was deputed from Indian Navy. I had the opportunity to interact with him and explain the offshore construction requirements and potential for India to enter offshore construction industry. He was keen in listening to me on few occasions whenever he was on board the barge Mahavir and showed interest in developing the Indian yard MDL with an offshore fleet, though it could not be expanded. Later, Mahavir barge itself was sold out. Capt. Mallapur was the captain of the barge and Mr. Deshpande the barge superintendent. Mr. Derrickboon was the diving superintendent from 2W, diving company.

Capt.Moghe was another captain who exchanged duty on the Mahavir on monthly basis. Capt. Mallapur was very knowledgeable on oceans and being jovial used to talk nicely and jokingly. Though offshore construction operations were new to him, he dealt with the operations very well. When a communication was conveyed from a diver at seabed which he could not understand he said, "My understanding is as clear as mud". Everyone had a laugh forgetting the seriousness of the issue with the technical problem. Later it was resolved, with everyone joining the discussion with ease. Why I bring out this example is that in offshore environment when everyone is under constant stress due to lack of social life, confined living and loneliness, this kind of approach to technical problems and issues get resolved with everyone's voluntary participation. Another time when a drilling rig in-charge was complaining about the sound created by the barge activities when some construction work was on-going adjacent to a drilling rig on operation, he jokingly said to the rig-in-charge, "You do not want us to take even a deep breath," and then the matter cooled down. I am writing these things to indicate how jovial nature is important to work successfully in offshore environments. Generally, after two weeks of stay in the sea, human behavior is affected, and even a depressive mind set is evolved. So, a good entertainment plan and good communication facilities to our homes and friends are essential to stay healthy at offshore/sea. Interaction with people onboard in a jovial and humorous way is required for a longer successful stay. Sailing in the sea continuously without touching land for a long time is really difficult. It makes people frustrated and depressed.

Coming to the immense requirement of barge Mahavir's support to complete the hook-up on HRA process complex for early flow of oil, a lot of discussions were held on board the barge to work out alternative ways for early flow of oil. I had a suggestion to the management that instead of waiting for commissioning of the HRA process complex for oil flow, the oil produced from the HA platform which is bridge connected to HRA could be directly sent to R-12 process complex, as well-fluid instead of processed crude oil for processing at R-12 as sufficient processing capacity was available at R-12 process platform. Production/Reservoir engineers were consulted along with other stake holders and the management agreed to the proposal. Shri.M.N.Madhahva, GM (C), Mr. P.V. Rao, GM (P) and Mr. E.Venugopal, project coordinator from ONGC supported the proposal and it was implemented successfully. MDL also came forward to undertake the temporary hook-up arrangements and safety measures at both ends HRA and R-12 as a free service as the delay in HRA commissioning was on their account contractually. This was successfully implemented in a matter of 2 weeks. It was a great achievement and the regular commissioning of HRA was done later at a normal pace. All this could happen mainly because the pipeline HRA R-12 was ready and in place. Here it is pertinent to mention the completion details of the HRA to R12 pipeline including burial of the pipeline. I was also present as ONGC representative most of the time on the pipeline barge and burial barge (jet barge) during laying of all HeeraPh-I pipelines, HA-HB, HA-HC and HRA-R12. The laying was smooth as the water depth in the area was small compared to Bombay High. Only during burial there was difficulty. Initially, a barge "Knight-Constructor" was deployed which could not carry out the sufficient burial depth using a Jet sled even after 2/3 passes of running over pipeline. The soil condition did not suit a Jet sled. Then it was discussed with experts and decided to mobilize a jet barge. The jetting methodology worked successfully, and the burial depth requirement of 1m cover was successfully achieved in a single pass by proper setting of Jet pressure and jet angle etc.

For the successful completion of the temporary flow to R-12, there was good support and backing from the management with least procedural formalities. In today's state of ONGC these achievements could be difficult to implement considering the compartmentalization of departments and procedural bottlenecks which have crept into the system after 2001 which I could feel when I returned from NIOT deputation. Temporary flow of well fluid directly from Heera to R-12 process complex was successfully done and was continued till regular commissioning and processing of crude was done at HRA process complex. When there is a will there is a way, even in disguise.

For the success of the implementation of oil flow from HA to R12 process platform 40km away, through the HA-HRA-bridge, HRA platform deck and then through a temporary hook up to riser of HRA-R12 (12") pipeline, Shri.Deshpande, MDL barge Mahavir's Construction Superintendent devoted his time day and night, for the erection and fabrication of spools for the temporary arrangements at site. I had one of the longest stays offshore at this time, at a stretch working 24 hours, only with few hours' sleep(nap) in between. Though the norms prescribed for offshore stay by ONGC is 14 days at a stretch, the persons who work for construction, stay longer and my stay was much longer than any of my colleagues. The happiness in contribution and success in implementation, overcoming difficulties was the driving force behind my enthusiasm for overstay. Also, I was a bachelor, so there was no family pressure as well to return to base. I should state here that around 200 days of my offshore compensatory offs (For 1 day in offshore 1 day compensatory off eligible), got lapsed, as I could not avail them when I got transferred to Chennai in 1991.

The oil flow was smooth as the diameter of the pipeline was large for well fluid flow, though longer distance of flow was to be done. The pressure drop was also negligible and reservoir engineers felt satisfied with the flow arrangement for even a few months without any constraint to future reservoir characteristics. At this time, as a reward for my contribution, GM© sent me to Mcdermott yard on deputation for fabrication supervision for a different project under him, in Dubai and Ras-Al-Kaimaa. Also at this time there was an invitation for me to join MNC at a lucrative salary, but I had to decline as a matter of principle.

2.3 HRA jacket installation- Avoided stand-by charges

I give below another incident which is worth sharing is produced below. At the time when HRA process platform jacket was installed, which was to be bridge connected to HA well platform, the drilling was on the verge of completion on HA. Knowing that the drilling rig was to move out of the HA platform during HRA jacket installation, a joint meeting at base office decided that the Derrick barge deployed for installation of the HRA jacket would move away from the location and be on stand-by at ONGC's cost during docking down and move away from the location by the drilling rig. A close co-ordination and interaction with the rig superintendent Shri. Velayudam was held for reducing the stand-by duration as much as possible for the barge so that the stand-by charges to be incurred by ONGC was minimum.

Being the ONGC representative on board the American's Derrick barge DB-14 installing the HRA jacket, I thought if there was a way out to save the standby charges by continuing the operations of the barge without a break while the drilling rig is moving out, why not make an attempt. The operation of jack up drilling rig move out involves pulling out the legs embedded into the seabed and bringing down the hull to float, while holding with three tug boats so that the hull does not hit the platform sideways. This is a coordinated careful movement/operation, which normally takes 8 to 12 hours.

My intuition to avoid the standby charges even for half a day was driving me to do something. I thought of attacking the prestige and expertise of American barge superintendent DB-14. I wrote a letter in advance to the barge superintendent, "We will advise you of the time of suspension of barge operations 6 hours in advance. However, we would appreciate it if you use your wisdom and expertise to continue the operations without interruptions by re-orienting the barge". This letter provoked his prestige and he talked to his base seeking clearance for re-orientation explaining its feasibility. He also sought clearance from ONGC to tie one nylon rope in lieu of one anchor line onto the jacket leg of HA platform towards additional safety and to avoid interference with the rig holding tugs and their holding lines. This methodology was agreed from all sides and finally implemented successfully without any standby of the barge. Infact, the rig took 2 ½ days to move out of location as one of the legs got stuck in the mud and took more time with jetting and other diver operations. A simple letter saved about US $ 200,000 to ONGC, at that time. I felt very satisfied though it may be a small saving for ONGC. It has become a practice for me to save, and innovate to economize in all my future assignments.

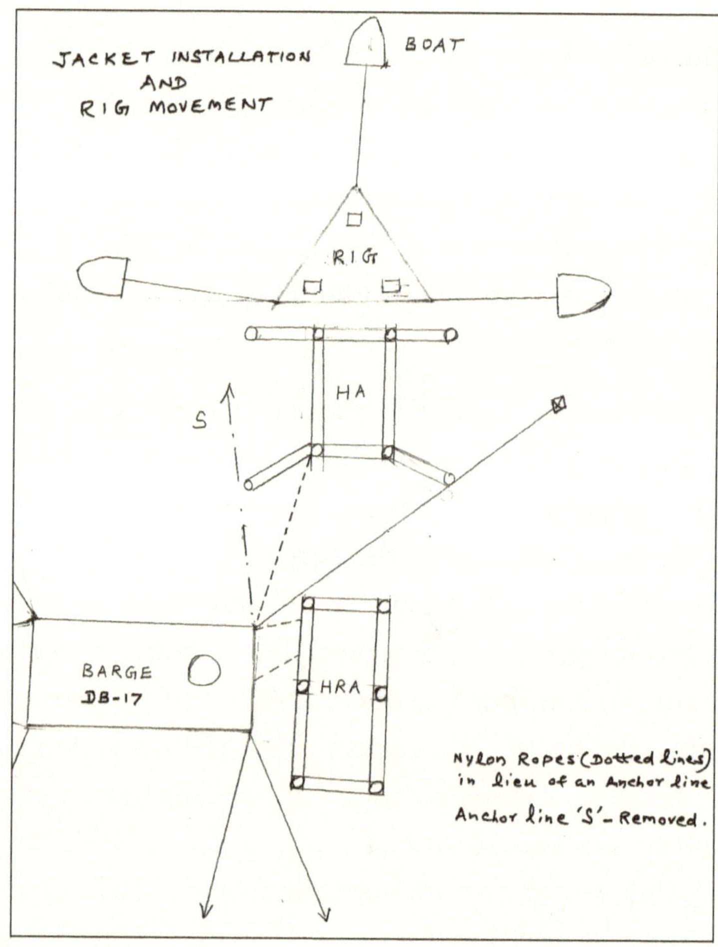

2.4 Accidents/ Mishaps at offshore

It is worth bringing out some of the mishaps/accidental happenings and bitter experiences in offshore Bombay High and Heera field to know how they were successfully overcome and to educate readers to avoid similar incidents with careful planning and precautions.

One such mishap was that one of the temporary buoyancy tanks attached to the jacket in the skirt legs came out of water while driving piles in the main legs like a bullet missile and hit the main crane of the construction barge. It was during installation of a well platform jacket fabricated by MDL and getting installed in Bombay High. They engaged the barge DLB crawler owned by Micoperi, an Italian company. After launching, towing to location, upending and placing the jacket structure onto the sea floor and then, while driving one set of main piles, one of the buoyancy tank got released due to vibrations and breaking of wedges/shims welded to hold the buoyancy tank. The attachment of additional buoyancy tank is sometimes required to have adequate reserve buoyancy for launching the jacket and required at least till upending and resting the jacket on its mud mat on the seabed. The buoyancy tank should have been punctured before driving the piles or adequate wedges/ shims welded properly to avoid such mishap.

This accident led to abrupt stoppage of the installation as the barge main crane boom broke and became inadequate for further use. The barge was demobilized, and another barge was sent to complete the installation.

Another incident that occurred during my stay on DLB crawler was a wet buckling of pipeline while laying an infield oil flow pipeline in Bombay High. The pipeline laying process offshore involves welding of 12m pieces of pipeline along the length of lay barge and lowering the pipeline to the seabed in a controlled manner through a stinger attached at the tail end of the barge. The pipeline welding is done in stages, X-rayed and then field coating done and sent through a tensioner for lowering. Every 8 to 10mins approximately 1 joint is completed and lowered. To speed up the process, every step is done at a quick pace, the field engineers work in shifts with no gap during working time. One of the weld's joint was X-ray cleared and pipe was allowed to be lowered by the contractor's field engineers as per his interpretation assuming it will be cleared. However, the QA Engineer from ONGC side did not accept the interpretation and advised to back-track the pipe for gouging and repair of the joint. For this the barge was to be moved back very carefully, however due to certain weather conditions the backing was not smooth, and the pipeline lost tension, and buckled (it became wet buckle). This was an unwarranted situation. It was a lengthy process to dewater the pipeline, pick-up again by deploying divers and start relaying after cutting the damaged length.

One more incident was while installing HA well platform jacket in Heera field. This time I was new, assisting the project coordinator, Mr. E. Venugopal in the field. When the jacket was launched, towed successfully to location and upending started before placing the jacket to seabed. Diver survey revealed that the end of the pipeline was just coming below the jacket. This is an infield pipeline coming from HB location to bring oil from that platform. The pipeline was already laid before jacket installation and maybe due to extra length laying or slight drifting of the pipeline, the end was coming below the jacket location coordinates. Options available were, either shift the location of jacket or cut the end of the pipeline and rectify later. As it was late at night and no timely, response was coming from base, project coordinator took a decision to cut the pipeline and proceed with the installation without any standby time to the barge awaiting decision.

Further to the above incidents I have two more important and lifesaving incidents to narrate. One was during hook-up works on one of the well platforms in Heera field with the support of MDL's barge Mahavir. The platform was connected to the barge with an inclined ladder arrangement and day and night hook-up and welding of piping works were ongoing. During one night around 2 AM, I was doing my rounds before going to sleep (this is the normal time I went to sleep on offshore duty, from 2 AM to 5 or 6 AM for 3 to 4 hrs). Usually, the DPR is sent to the base by 7 a.m. ONGC representatives on construction barges have 24 hours duty. No specific time to rest. Generally, the work is sluggish from 2/3 AM to 5/6 AM while from 6 AM to 2 AM the next morning good speed of work is observed, though people work in shifts.

Coming to the incident, after reaching the platform through the ladder from the barge, I heard some sound coming from the water level, which was a man's feeble voice. With 50% doubt, I shouted and called the nearby people to bring a torch light and check below the jacket level. It was found that one rigger had slipped and fallen into the water and was holding the conductor pipes. He was unable to raise a loud or voice, above the sound of the waves which was loud. Immediately, a diver was sent for his rescue, and he was safely taken back to the barge. He was very lucky to get saved as that area was prone to movement of sharks. We thanked God. The rigger was allowed to return to base and take rest for a few days to overcome his fearful state.

Another accident I witnessed during my stay at offshore construction barge as ONGC representative was injury to an EIL engineer who was posted in HSL yard Vizag and had come to Bombay High for inspection during installation. After installation of the jacket was almost complete the 30" drilling conductors were to be installed onto the jacket through the conductor guides along the jacket length at various levels. This was to save the drilling rig time to erect the conductors before commencement of drilling. Earlier these were installed by the drilling rig, which was diverted to a construction group. Though there are advantages and disadvantages this arrangement was decided by the management.

While one of the conductors was welded on the barge with two pieces of prefabricated conductors and lifted and lowered into the slot it was getting stuck at the 2nd level below the water surface. The contractor argued that the conductor guides were not in line but eccentric, hence not going into it. But EIL engineer was very confident that the alignment was very carefully checked at the fabrication yard, and it was correct. The welding on board the barge was skewed, and the joined conductor pipe was not straight, that was the reason it is not going through, as per the EIL engineer. I was to take a decision whether the conductor pipe was to be taken back, cut the weld and re-align the joint and re-weld. If it passes through this time, with the new weld, the entire time of the barge and cost was to contractor's account. Otherwise, it was to ONGC's account. Hence if the re-weld also failed, the conductor could not be put forever, and one slot would be lost. Otherwise also if we decided now to abandon the lowering of this conductor, at least we could save the barge cost for the re-trial.

I took a calculated risk and decided to go for the re-weld & re-install the conductor, which came out successful. Though technically it was a good decision, unfortunately, it led to an accident injuring the EIL engineer.

This happened when the conductor pipe pieces were re-welded on the construction barge Mahavir. As there was space constraint on the barge deck, this alignment was kept close to another string of parallel pipes. On that fateful night the weather was rough leading to more rolling of the barge. During one such roll, the pipe rolled on the supports overcoming the wedges provided and hit the EIL engineer who was standing in between the two pipe strings, checking the alignment of the concerned pipe string. It hit the private parts of the engineer and he was bleeding. He was taken to the emergency treatment room and the captain himself gave first aid and stopped the bleeding. But he was in severe pain and trauma, so I called for an emergency chopper from BHN offshore platform complex. As it was night time the chopper pilot refused to land on the helideck of the barge was the elevation of the helideck on the barge was very close to the water level and not as in a platform complex. Then we shifted the patient along with an escort by a boat to BHN complex, Where he was lifted to the platform by a basket and airlifted to a Bombay hospital and got admitted in the night within a few hours. Though he had some permanent setbacks, his life was saved and resumed duty in an office environment till his retirement.

2.5   HD/HE well platforms project-Innovations

After the phase-I works of Heera field executed by MDL were completed, the ICB tendering was taken up for two additional well platforms HD and HE. MDL installed HA, HB, and HC well platforms, HRA process complex, HRA-R12 pipeline and infield well fluid pipelines. HD/HE well platform project was awarded to

Nippon Steel Corporation, Japan. The project was awarded at just 18MM US $, which was then very cheap, and the project group got appreciation from the management. The design work was done at Tokyo, NSC design office and fabrication works were done at NSC's Wakamatsu fabrication yard. I had the opportunity to visit both places for design review & fabrication supervision.

I had travelled by Air India from Bombay to Tokyo via Delhi, Calcutta, Hongkong, Osaka. It was a tedious journey, though it was my second international travel, first one being to Dubai. This had taken more time and was more tiresome with no proper sleep. When I got down at Tokyo, I was fully exhausted. The person who was to receive me at the airport left, as the immigration and other clearances took more time. I had to travel by limousine bus to reach my hotel where my accommodation was booked. It was night and I went to eat in a nearby Indian restaurant with an ONGC colleague who was already present there, Shri. A. Mukherjee, whom I was supposed to relieve.

After completion of design review at NSC design office Tokyo, I moved to Wakamatsu fabrication yard as fabrication works commenced there.

At the design review office, the exchange of documents and review comments incorporation were smooth. EIL engineering coordinator Mr. R.Sundar and ONGC's E & P wing representatives were all supportive for a fast review and quick finalization of purchase specs at record time with day-by-day monitoring of all documents, drawings, status and actions required for completion.

At the fabrication yard NSC management proposed to use steel which was older than two years and submitted documents supporting all strength criteria physically and qualitatively, meeting all test requirements and specifications. As ONGC representative, I refused to accept the deviation from our specifications in the bid package and insisted that NSC use new steel less than 2 years old meeting the design criteria. NSC agreed to the same finally though initially tried their best to substitute the old steel even proposing some remedial measures/favours. I was stubborn with my decision and succeeded in my verdict while all external pressures fizzled out as I sent written messages to all concerned on my verdict without any time lag.

During the visit to NSC's design office in Tokyo, I had the opportunity to visit a few places in Tokyo, like Tokyo Tower, Disneyland etc. I also visited a few Indian restaurants to have Indian food and travelled in their underground trains. It was a nice experience and travel to any place was easy, with the colour coding of train routes and change over at junctions where two routes meet.

During the stay at Wakamatsu fabrication yard, I stayed in a hotel at Kokura. From here, one Sunday I visited the atom bombed location of Hiroshima by Shinkansen express train. It was a very fast train, and I had the thrill of travelling at such high speed for the first time. It was a great surprise to see Hiroshima city had been developed so nicely and beautifully and could not believe that the city was destroyed by an atom bomb. The hard work of the Japanese people and their sincerity to the nation could be felt everywhere during my visit to Japan.

During the offshore installation works at HD/HE, I stayed most of the time offshore in their barge and successfully completed the project. With this Heera phase-I was complete. The production was more than projected and the management was pleased with the achieved milestones.

It is worth writing about the offshore planning, scheduling and execution of the installation and pre-commissioning activities of HD, HE platforms and the pipelines by NSC, Japan. Their construction barge Kuroshio-1 was used for offshore installation works where I was stationed till completion and handing over of the platforms to the production department of ONGC.

Their meticulous planning and detailing of works offshore helped in completion of works at a short time compared to other installation contractors. They even noted the small details of existing interface platform facilities so that the modification and interface with existing platforms with their new HD/HE platforms was smooth and without any delay.

The project manager from NSC Mr. Yamamoto's approach and meticulous planning and timely implementation is to be appreciated.

Based on the experience with the MDL platforms, certain innovations were done on HD/HE platforms configurations which paved the way for economization of offshore field developments. Infact, a preliminary presentation was made to the then member (offshore), Dr. A.K.Malhotra and he approved in principle to go ahead with the ideas/innovations.

One of the reasons for innovation was MDL's delay in procurement of long lead equipment and one such equipment was the test separator on well platforms. When the main deck and helideck of HB and HC platforms could not be loaded out for offshore installation for want of erection of test separators it was decided to load out and install them without test separators and install the test separators later when they arrived.

This decision led to installing the equipment as an independent item and even in very calm weather, it was extremely difficult to install the test separators as its location was on the side of cellar deck. The main deck is the top deck surface which is free and installation of any equipment on main deck(top deck) is relatively easy as a separate lift for offshore installation Though the separators were installed with difficulty on HB/HC platforms with some damage to the decks and separator parts, it paved the way for a new thinking and innovative deck layout. The equipment layout of cellar deck and main deck were rearranged leading to efficient deck layout, re-orientation of fire water pump, test separator to main deck, crane mount location to a new place thereby enabling 360° rotation of crane with access to all deck areas which was earlier limited to only 240°. This was successfully implemented in HD/HE well platforms. Mr. B.Ghosh of EIL was kind enough to incorporate these innovations and modify the structural design accordingly.

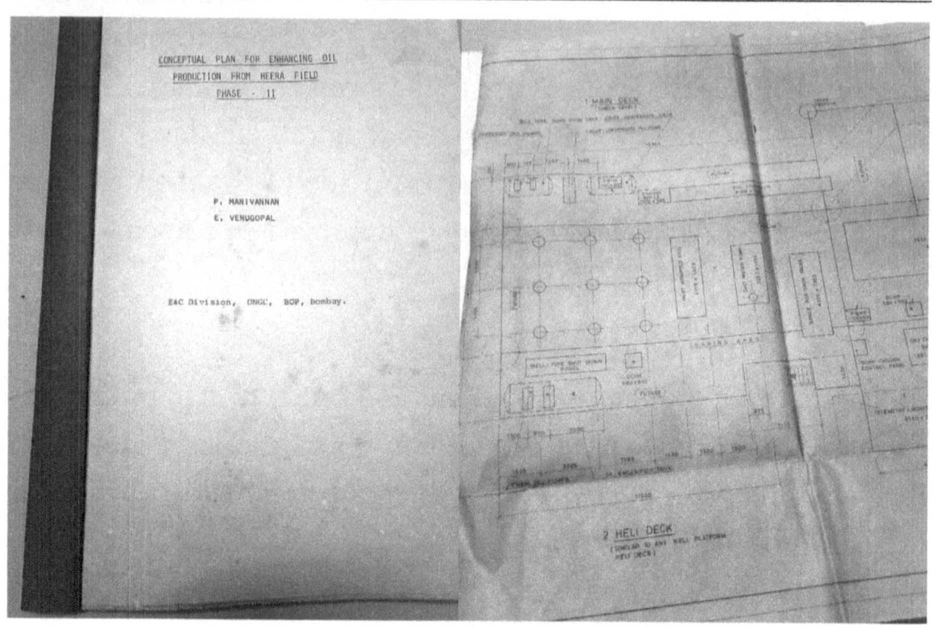

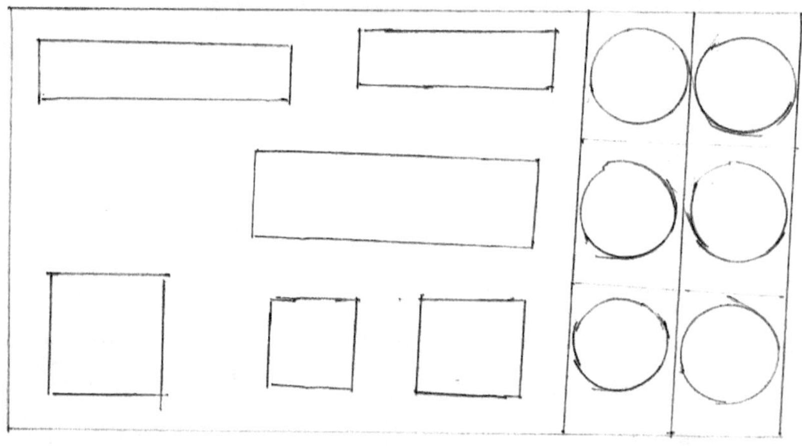

OLD DESIGN
-6 SLOTS

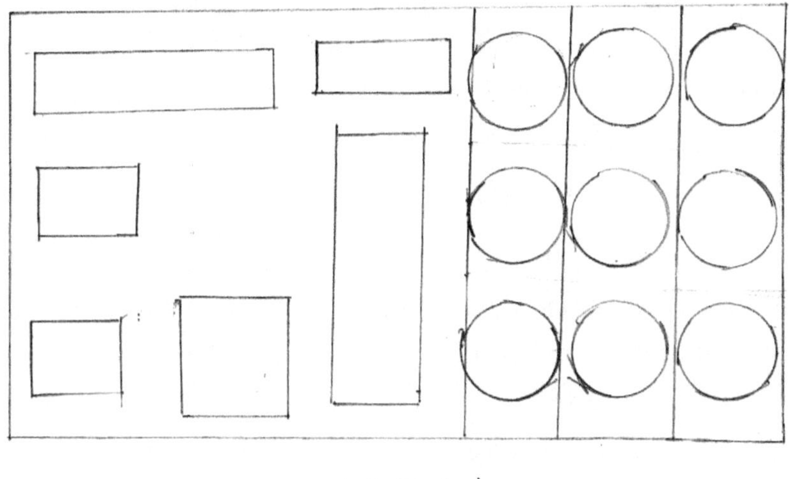

Further, this revised layout helped in allotting one more row of well slots (i.e., 3 more well slots) in the well platforms design thereby a well platform can have 9 well slots instead of the 6 slots in all previous well platforms installed in Bombay High at little or no extra cost.

This concept was incorporated in HQRSTF well platforms planning later under Heera Phase-II development. Adding three wells to a platform is saving half of a platform cost (2 platforms instead of 3) in a field development. Now, even 12 slots well platforms are designed and installed, with the forerunner being HD/HE well platforms.

The engineering and planning department generally take up innovations and various options towards economization of field development; however the present innovation was devised and implemented by the project group with the active support of the Heera project coordinator of ONGC Mr. E. Venugopal, and I am grateful for his encouragement in incorporating the innovations. Dr. S.K. Malhotra, Member (offshore) who had originally approved the proposal was not there to appreciate these implementations. He had to leave ONGC as the post of Member (offshore), was abolished and he left to join the World-Bank.

The CMD brought in a new organizational structure, namely business group concept which also worked very well with distribution of power amongst more Directors than the earlier concept of only Member(offshore) and Member(onshore).New posts of directors in drilling, production, exploration, and technical were created and this concept successfully ran the organization till 2001.

* * *

Chapter 3

HEERA PH-II Development

Coming to the further course of my journey in ONGC, I took up the supportive role in preparation of feasibility report, taking approval/sanction from ONGC board, CCEA clearance, division of phase-II work of the Heera field development with Mr. E. Venugopal who was my great support in all my pro-active approach towards the given assignment to the group. The work I had to undertake were interactions with engineering and planning department of ONGC, operation business group engineers i.e., production engineers, exploration and reservoir engineers, collect inputs for design and cost estimates for the project. Also, more interactions were held with EIL who were the design engineering consultants for the project. It is pertinent that we had interaction and good support from stalwarts like Dr. S. Ramanathan, Shri.P.K.Ramasamy, Shri.P.V.Rao and Shri.N.K. Mitra of ONGC for the Heera project, whenever I visited them in their offices, in connection with Heera Ph-II development.

Heera phase-II was sanctioned with three division of projects:

1) WIH-HRG process platform complex.
2) HQRSTF, five well platforms and associated well-fluid pipelines.
3) Heera to Uran trunk pipeline.

The project group which worked for the sanction, division of work and preparation of the three group of bid packages was hopeful of executing the primary division of the process complex and collating the other two divisions to two other groups for parallel execution.

Unfortunately, due to some other interests of people in the E & C division, key projects were taken (i.e., projects of foreign contract execution) by another group and well platforms & pipelines which were contracted to Indian yards were assigned to the original group which brought out the development by the local management at Bombay.

* * *

Chapter 4

Infill platforms, Bombay High

At this juncture, I was transferred to another group and got associated with a completely new project, infill platforms project, IE/IL and BH22/BH25 (WA/WB) contracted to M/S Hindustan Shipyard Ltd. The project coordinator Mr. P.N.Karkal was new to ONGC who was posted directly at a senior level with his experience in offshore works abroad in the US. It was a great pleasure working with him. Whereas I could learn many things from his experience, he was dependent on my experience in ONGC to understand the system and variances of ONGC procedures. It was at this time I took almost the role of the project coordinator taking up all the responsibilities of the project jointly with Mr. P.N.Karkal. The design (detailed engineering) was done at EIL, New Delhi. Fabrication work was done at Hindustan Shipyard Vizag. I was deployed at both the centers most of the time. I was given special approval by CMD to travel by air for domestic travel to Delhi, Vizag etc. though I was not entitled to travel by air considering my position in ONGC at that time. It was challenging to get the work completed as per schedule, as HSL had little experience in offshore structures.

Once, one of the jacket structures(BH-25) was almost ready to load out, but for the fit-out of the sump caisson, a long lead item, to complete the jacket for load-out. Installing the jacket before monsoon (i.e., before May) and giving it for drilling with a temporary deck would advance the oil flow by one year as the drilling rig was already available. I suggested to the management and Shri S.K.Goyal, then GM (C&M), that the jacket could be loaded out and installed without sump caisson by providing a clamped arrangement for future offshore installation of sump caisson instead of a welded sump caisson support. This was accepted after a while; the jacket was loaded out almost close to the onset of monsoon.

Again, the installation became a challenge before monsoon and somehow completed (of course with some compromises) without compromising on structural safety. Some of the instant decisions made into the work for successful timely installation were, in-complete grouting of main legs and skirt legs, part driving of conductors(remaining was left to the drilling rig to take up) etc. Dr. Hariharan's(EIL) timely check of structural adequacy with the above compromises for a season helped in decision making and success. Offshore work is full of challenges and the happiness you derive on overcoming the challenge and succeed is thrilling and wonderful. It is in this BH-22/25 platforms that the first subsea wells in Bombay High were planned to be connected and provisions were made on these platforms.

HSL, though new to offshore platforms, had done a wonderful job, except for the delay in execution of the project, the quality of work was comparable to any International fabrication yard.

HSL got more orders from ONGC, and they were awarded with the work of Ravva project offshore works phase-I also in modular form. Ravva-10, Ravva-17 platforms and their pipelines were awarded to them after IE/IL/WA/WB project. BH-22 and BH-25 were renamed as WA and WB.

When I was coordinating the work of IE/IL/BH-22/BH-25 from Bombay E & C division, the Southern Region of ONGC awarded the Ravva project work to HSL and the ONGC team from the Southern Region was also stationed at Vizag fabrication yard. It was very hectic for HSL and ONGC technical teams in the HSL offshore yard. As HSL and their subcontractors were new to offshore structures, ONGC and EIL engineers had to guide them in the day-to-day activities of fabrication. M/S Techsharp and M/S Bhageeratha Engineering were of very good support to HSL as subcontractors in fabrication.

4.1 New construction technique for reduction in Mud-mat weight Of offshore platforms

It was during this time, I invented a new construction technique for reduction in mud-mat weight of offshore platforms. The technique and the innovation were presented to the then Member(Tech) Shri.S.K.Manglik who later became CMD, ONGC. He appreciated the innovation and advised ONGC to PATENT the technique as an ONGC patent which was taken up by ONGC. The idea for this innovation came from my appreciation of a grouting technique, first innovated and patented by an engineer who then became an entrepreneur with his technique.

Pressure grouting is an alternative to conventional grouting method of jacket legs with piles. Details are available in OTC-conference paper 2082 of 1974. Briefly, after driving the piles into seabed through the jacket legs, the annulus between the jacket legs and piles is grouted with cement pumping, for integrity to transfer the platform loads to the piles. This is done after inflating the diaphragms pre-fitted at the bottom of the jacket legs for sealing from water ingress from bottom and to avoid diluting the cement. Cement is filled from the bottom of the leg and rises above in the annulus.

Against the above conventional method, this entrepreneur devised that by initially applying air pressure from the top of the annulus, water could be driven out from the annulus. Now, while withdrawing the air pressure, we could slowly pump in cement. In this process we could fill cement to about half of the annulus against the outside water pressure in lieu of the cement density vs sea water density.

I was very enthused about this technique, and was always dreaming of an innovation with buoyancy, water pressure and other parameters and the reduction in mud mat technique was born out of this entrepreneur's success on pressure grouting.

A technical paper was sent to ISOPE for oral presentation in ISOPE-91 at Edinburg. Due to foreign travel restrictions, although we could not travel to Edinburg for presentation, the paper was published in Isope-91 which could be searched and found in Google even now. Shri.R.M. Kotresh a colleague of mine, a civil engineer assisted me in the geo-technical calculations and quantification of the reduction in mud-mat weight by this innovative technique. In brief, the technique is to make the lead sections of the piles buoyant while stabbing them initially onto the jacket legs before driving the piles into seabed thereby the load carrying capacity required for the mud mat is reduced. It was deduced that approximately 30% of the mud mat weight could be saved and in certain cases we could even switch over to wooden mud mat. Also, any reduction in mud mat steel reduces the cathodic protection requirement for the jacket resulting in more cost saving to the structures.

A merit award was proposed to be given during Republic Day for the innovation, but during the approval, the Head of E & C division at that time directed that the award be given only after implementation, which never happened.

* * *

Chapter 5

Engineering and Planning Division, Bombay

With the background and my experience in various offshore activities and exposure to problem-solving as base coordinator for offshore installation monitoring works of a group headed by Mr. M.N.Madhava, I was recruited into the engineering and planning section. In a very short time after moving into E & P division, I proposed to take up design review, fabrication/ installation supervision by ONGC engineers. To support this, only certification services were proposed to be taken from a third-party certification agency. I prepared a bid package for the selection of a third-party certification agency and M/S MECON was selected by ONGC for the same. Shri Binod Chandra, General Manager(E&P), had extended total support in this venture.

While in E & P division, I coordinated to compile general specifications, applicable codes, and standards for ready reference to engineers in the discipline in all the areas. At this time, I had a close association with the Institutes IEOT (Institute of Engineering and

Ocean Technology) and developed a synergy with Engineering and Planning dept and this helped in strengthening the E & P division to evolve as alternative to EIL in all the areas of offshore works so as to become almost independent with the least support from consultants.

Also, at this time various thumb rule formulae were worked out with other colleagues for use in project cost estimation, like installed cost of jacket $/Ton, piles $/Ton, topside $/ton, pipeline cost per inch dia. etc. I sometimes checked these thumb rules with some project costs after 10-15 years and they still matched. The cost of an offshore pipeline at 50 $/inch.m works out correct even today. Though I worked for only a very short time in E &P Bombay, with the experience acquired at E&C and E&P, I continued the same work later in Chennai. The thumb rule estimate figures, even helped me quickly, in giving an independent opinion sometime in 2007/8 sought by a senior executive of a company, whether they can venture into a Mega project called KALPASAR in Gujarat, for which NIOT had done extensive survey, on commercial aspects as well, apart from pure technical opinion.

This start-up of engineering review, fabrication, installation supervision without EIL(consultant) became a routine in due course of time at ONGC.

This experience and exposure helped in handling the GS-15/23 project in East Coast without EIL(consultant), independently by ONGC team of engineers and I could successfully co-ordinate and complete the GS-15/23 project later in the East Coast, the forerunner for the present prestigious Eastern offshore Asset of ONGC at Kakinada.

* * *

Chapter 6

E & C Division, Chennai

In 1990 May, I got married and took my spouse to Bombay. As she could not appreciate and adjust to life at Bombay, I decided to move to Chennai/Karaikal. Fortunately, I got transferred to Chennai and joined the E & C division there and became part of the Ravva project from June 91.

6.1   RV-10 and RV-17 Installation challenges

The installation of the RV-10 and RV-17 platforms (the very first platforms of East Coast, India) were supervised at offshore by me along with Shri.S.P.Muthukaruppan and a few others. Both the platforms were successfully installed by McDermott International. However, there was an issue in pulling the flexible riser pipe(supplied by Coflexip, France) to carry oil & gas from the well through the J-tube of the platform which was an integral part of the yard fabrication. The pulling failed as the stub-end could not pass through the bend of the J-tube and the pulling winch line snapped at 90 T force. By reviewing the drawings and the fabrication methodology it was found that the curved portion of the J-tube designed by EIL, was made-up of miter joints instead of a smooth curve in the yard by HSL, due to which the stub-end of the flexible riser got stuck in the miter welds.

The operation was abandoned, and I proceeded to the base to discuss with senior officials to find a solution. Shri.C.K.Srinivasan, the General Manager, was under tremendous pressure from the management for scheduled completion for oil flow. I sat down with Mr. M.Thyagaraj, Chief Engineer, till late at night in the office and worked out a solution. A sketch was made for fabrication of an I-tube (in lieu of J) segment and J segment separately. The J segment was built up by two split halves to reel-in flexible pipe so that no pulling effort is required. This innovative concept was welcomed by all agencies involved and it was decided to fabricate and mobilize them to offshore. It was re-engineered to pre-fix the flexible riser into the I-tube and clamp the two halves of the split J segment to the I-Tube section along with flexible riser onto the platform like conventional riser installation. This was successfully implemented in a short time with the support of HSL, EIL and the installation contractor.

There was another issue joining the shore portion of pipeline and deeper portion of pipeline by a welded joint as per design, due to limitations of the barge used for the pipeline tie-in. M/S Essar was the installation contractor and Scanlay was the barge used.

The Scanlay barge being a small hook-up barge, the number of side davits for lifting two pipeline segments and welding them on the barge by proper alignment was not technically feasible as available davits for each pipeline segments was insufficient to bring the face of ends parallel to each other for welding and then lower them to the seabed. A longer lay barge would have been suitable for this operation, as this was not known until the job was taken up and mobilizing a suitable barge at this time was not practically possible. Otherwise, we had to wait for one more working season that would delay the oil flow by about one year which was unacceptable.

Here again the General Manager was under tremendous pressure as the deadline for oil flow was nearing. I had suggested fitting 900 # class full bore flanges at each end of the pipeline segments by individually lifting them to the surface and welding the flange, lowering them back to seabed, then bringing the flanges together and bolting them with divers. This was the only option feasible at that time to catch up with the schedule of oil flow. After taking clearance from EIL for engineering details and the adequacy for the change, the work was successfully done.

Yet another testing time was while pigging the pipeline from offshore platform side Pig-launcher with a scrapper Pig. The Pig was launched into the barrel and pumping started. Even after more than 12 hours, the Pig was not received at the receiver end at the onshore terminal, but water was coming continuously at full flow rate. Everyone was giving different theories with no solution. As I had a similar experience in a Bombay High pipeline pigging where the Pig was stuck at the launcher barrel itself in a tilted position at the T-point allowing the water to flow after stopping water pumping, opening the barrel, it was found that the same fate had happened to this Pig also. Later this was completed successfully, ensuring the successful passing of the pig through the flange joint in the mid-sea. Further hydrotest also was successfully done.

However, oil flow was done without burial of the pipeline, which (burial of pipeline) was also a requirement as per design criteria. M/S Essar agreed to complete the burial after the monsoon. With this commitment oil flow from RV-17 commenced and later on from RV-10.

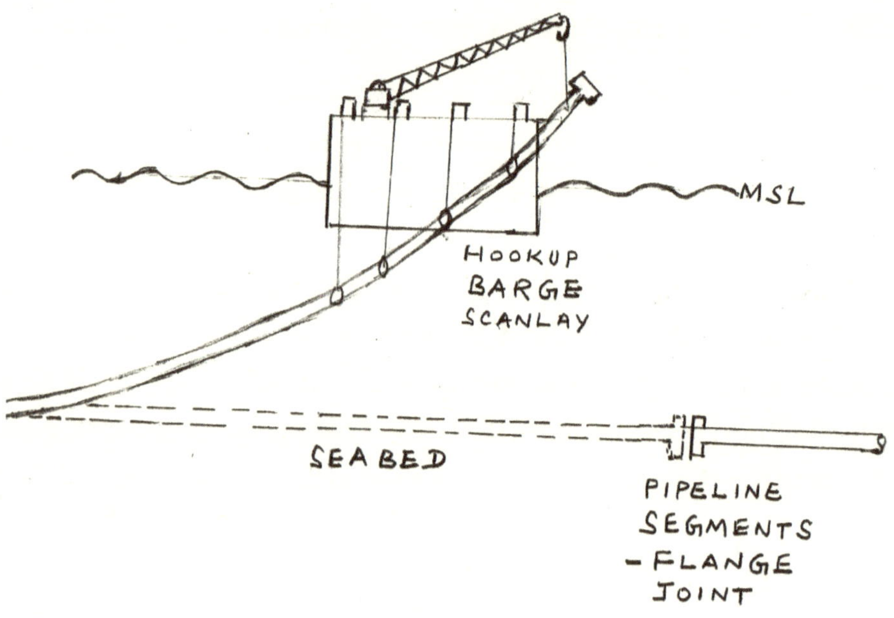

M/S Essar could not take up burial of the pipelines by mobilizing a burial barge in the next working season also. A survey was conducted to see the condition of the pipelines. It was found out that the pipelines were flush buried by self-weight and monsoon action. Stability analysis carried out with pipelines in flush buried condition revealed that the pipelines are stable. Later it was decided that the scope of work of burial of the pipelines was removed from the contract and the contract concluded saving the cost of burial. This fait-accompli situation led to an innovative design concept in the next shallow water development project of ONGC, GS-15/23 platform project for application of a new design concept towards pipeline stability, namely "Self-burial of pipelines" and successfully implemented as a cost cutting measure in the GS-15/23 offshore marginal field development project in the East coast.

During this time, when the success story of GS-15/23 spread across ONGC up to the top management, a team of engineers from E & C Division, Bombay was deputed to Chennai to study the features and concepts like, monopile, self-burial, inclusion of scope of work of certification under contractor's scope etc., towards cost cutting and later applied in their projects.

As the Ravva phase-I was concluding in E & C division, Chennai, advance actions were taken for phase-II works and tenders were floated for Ravva phase-II by E and C division Chennai. Daily meetings with bidders were held, one bidder a day, discussing and resolving the techno commercial deviations raised by bidders and I was associated mostly with the technical part. Everyday meetings and signing of minutes on the same day went up to even 8-9 pm.

One day, with one bidder, though all technical deviations were resolved, one commercial issue was not getting resolved till 9 pm in the night. I entered the commercial meeting and within 10 minutes the matter was resolved and concluded and in another half an hour all went home. Briefly I will bring it out for the benefit of readers. The bidder's deviation was that he had not considered the cost of second mobilization to complete the project in case of any delay due to adverse monsoon, weather window changes, company directions etc and company shall compensate for that. It was vague, and tough arguments were put forth from the bidder's side and ONGC side and no resolution could be arrived. I suggested that "The bidder has informed that his quote is based on single mobilization; noted by the company. Bidder withdraws his deviation/clarification raised" as a resolution in the minutes and everyone agreed. GM(ONGC) and senior executive from the bidder, both appreciated this simple resolution, understanding the crux that it will take care of the interests of both in future, if he ever became the successful contractor; there was no need to break our heads then. All pros and cons of the resolution were analyzed and agreed to, within a few minutes. I have brought out this example to emphasize why timely and quick decisions are relevant in projects. Many such incidents were there in my career, though I could not record everything here.

At a critical stage, just before evaluation of bids, EBG group of ONGC advised E & C division not to proceed with the tender for phase-II, citing review of reserves estimated by them. This was a shock to E & C and as advised by them, phase-II was abandoned. Soon after that, Government of India's new Policy of privatizing oil fields through Joint ventures with private firms, was announced and Ravva field was handed over to Command Petroleum, Australia. This company later developed this field as earlier planned by ONGC under phase-II with no changes at all. Readers may ask why the scheme had not undergone any change if the reservoir estimates were redone. We know what happened further and the glorious Ravva field was taken over by private parties and later operated by Cairn energy with some ONGC experts leaving and joining them. Col. S.P. Wahi in his book "Leading from the Front " mentioned "It is a great pity that this field was donated to a little known operator..."

6.2 Joint Venture Participation

I was deputed to Australia for the technical review of the bids received against Ravva phase-II by Command Petroleum, ONGC being a JV Partner. The bid package floated by Command Petroleum was not an engineered one and only the design inputs and requirements were spelt out. This was completely different from the policy of ONGC where our bids are basic engineered with design criteria, specifications, drawings including codes and standards to be followed with clear terms. I have a strong opinion that a basic engineered bid package is a must to get the best facilities at a competitive price.

Though I was against this concept by the JV, I could not do much, but only limit my review findings which were conveyed to the JV for incorporation and was welcomed by the JV. One major change proposed by me was to have the RC platform bridge connected to RA, instead of having a platform at 1 km distance. This saved a pipeline and a helideck. This idea was conceived as a corollary to the proposal of adding a clamp-on well slot to RA platform and studied for feasibility with guidance from Mr. M. Thyagaraj to increase oil flow. Later this concept spread to old well platforms in Bombay high for additional clamp-on well slots.

Many other technical comments given by me and our team (One finance rep, one production expert and myself) were conveyed to bidders for compliance. The price bid when opened was a great surprise to all JV partners. But I was not surprised as the root cause was that the bid package was not engineered. All bidders cannot put in reasonable engineering effort to arrive at the best contract price as it involves cost and time. More guestimates had gone into their estimates leading to variation of contract price two-fold, the highest price being double the lowest price which is uncommon. An engineered package will not bring this much variation in prices. Also going to the lowest bidder, we may not get the right process scheme, facilities, and best quality. This happened as I predicted. The disadvantages are multifold. As mentioned above we get a lower efficient process scheme, facilities etc. from a contractor with poor workmanship and also as he will be shrewd in quoting a bigger price as he is aware that other bidders would not come closer to him, in lieu of their standard with their sound engineering practices. Also there would be long term losses due to extra maintenance. This was my argument.

Many discussions were held as to whether to go to L2 or L3 for better scheme, quality etc., but finally it emerged that L1 only would have to be awarded the contract which matched the fit for purpose criteria, as given in the bid package. M/S HHI became the successful contractor who executed Ravva Phase-II and we all know the later successful story of the Ravva field. Even today it is producing as one of the best oil fields in the Eastern offshore.

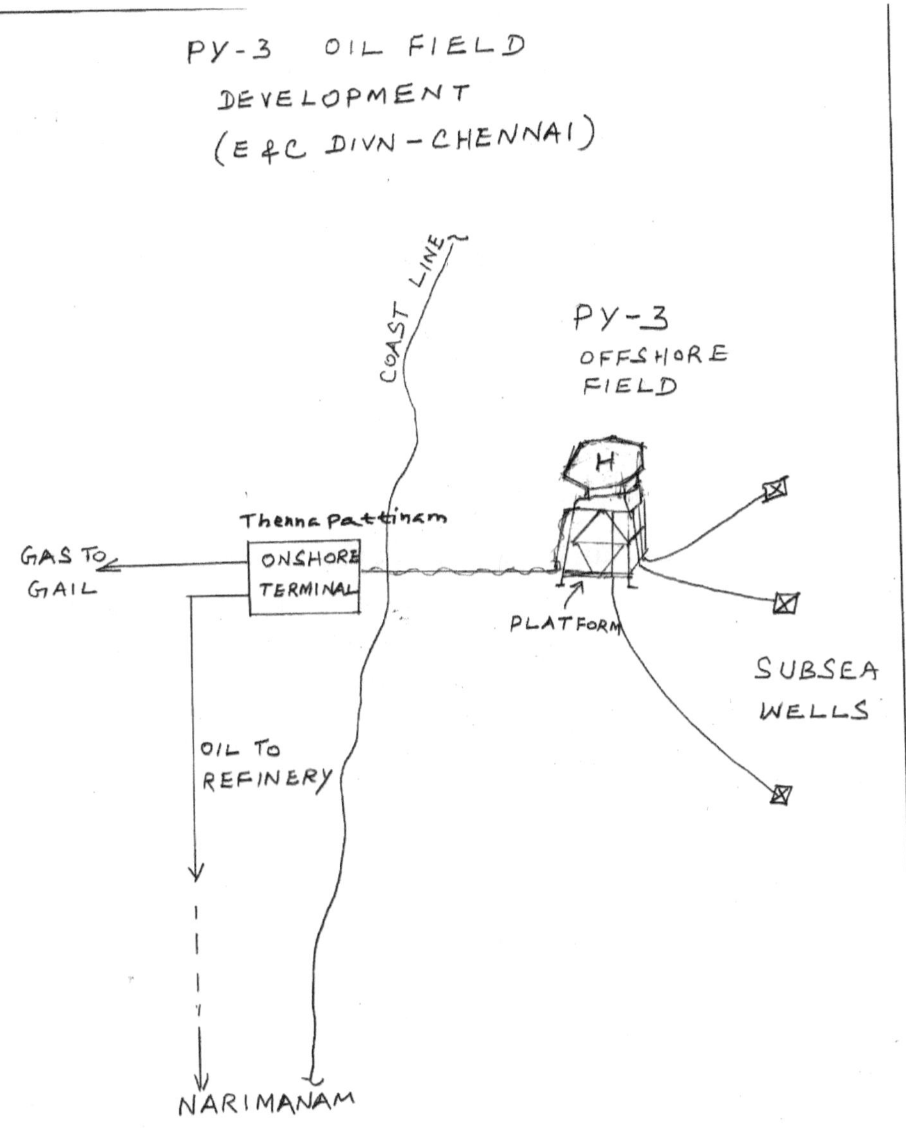

I was associated as a technical member in the operating committee of the JV's awarded in the east coast. I was also participating in the JV meetings of PY-3 field awarded to a JV operated by Hardy Oil. When the development plan options were discussed, I objected to the operator's plan of production through a floating production system (FPSO Tahara) by hiring the facilities with subsea completion of wells. I suggested putting a well platform in one of the well locations at about 50-80metre water depth and completing the wells by subsea completion. After collecting the oil at the well platform, flow the combined well fluid to landfall point nearest to the well platform. Thennapattinam was the ideal land terminal location. After processing at the terminal, the associated gas could be sold to GAIL at the terminal point. The produced oil could be transported by a land pipeline to Panangudi Refinery which was coming up there. My argument was that the operator's proposal would lead to burning of associated gas which may be substantial in due course of production, when GOR (Gas Oil Ratio) increases thereby losing a huge revenue. Another drawback of the operator's proposal was that the field production had to be stopped when the revenue from the field was equal to hiring cost plus operating cost. Whereas in the case of well platform and land terminal the field can be operated to extract maximum oil with low operating cost. The higher CAPEX in putting up the platform and terminal can be easily offset by many years of extended production through this option with addional gas revenue which was burnt.

I made a written comment advising ONGC not to agree to the operator's scheme of development. But unfortunately, a decision was taken by the management committee in favor of the operator. This proved to be a disaster later as predicted by me. The field produced for about 12 years and had to shut down due to non-sustainable commercial viability and related controversies between JV partners, as predicted. Multiples of thousands of crores (I am not a reservoir engineer to estimate) worth of oil gets locked up in the reservoir which was not extracted and as per the platform based production strategy, atleast upto 2040, the oil production could have sustained with huge revenue to Govt. and ONGC, leave alone the cut we had to share with private players which otherwise would have entirely come to ONGC and Govt. I was informed by one of my old colleagues in ONGC who switched over to Hardy-Oil later that the operator realized the mistake of not going with the scheme I suggested, and a senior executive of Hardy oil even recollected my comment in the JV operating committee. What is the use of repenting later? As mentioned else-where, my opinion, why should national wealth be ever handed over to MNC's for exploitation, this example will prove my point, as they will be interested to encash maximum profit in a shorter period and there will be no consideration for long term energy security of the country which was the agenda for privatization/globalization of oil exploration and production. No doubt, for a country with just 0.5% of world oil resources and demand for oil increasing exponentially, globalization will not resolve oil security but will only deteriorate it, with more and more shortfall in future. It is a pity why policy makers could not look at this point instead of continuing with the same strategy. Any revival of Py-3 oilfield development should be on long term sustenance rather than short term goals.

6.3 GS-15/23 Offshore Marginal Field Development

After completion of Ravva project, there was no techno commercially viable project in the East Coast for ONGC to develop. At this juncture, many officers of E & C division got transferred and some retired. I was left in the section with very few people. Myself, under the guidance of Shri.M.Thyagaraj, the then Chief Engineer (who later retired from ONGC as Executive Director) undertook many studies for the development of marginal offshore fields with innovative concepts towards cost reduction & light weight offshore platforms instead of conventional well platforms. After the transfer of Mr. Thyagaraj to the eastern region, I followed up the strategy of cost-effective platforms for GS-15/23 and finally evolved a scheme. Mr. E. Venugopal and subsequently Mr. H.Sridhara, joined the section at a senior level during the implementation of the most economical, cost-effective GS-15/23 offshore marginal field project with one of the world's smallest oil platforms. Sleipneir, reported as one of the world's smallest oil platforms, constructed in the port of Rotterdam for Dana Petroleum installed in Oct 2020 weighed 395 tonnes, while, GS-15 is around 320 tonnes only.

Though I was in the middle level in this project, the entire hierarchy of the management up to the ONGC board was satisfied to accept the innovative concepts and ideas put up by me towards the successful implementation.

The project was conceived with bare minimum top side facilities on the monopile platform with pipelines self-burial concept.

It was conceived that two exploratory wells GS-15-4 and GS-23-1 would be developed with monopile platforms at these locations. A 4-inch dia pipeline from GS-23-1 would flow the gas to GS-15-4 location and a 6-inch dia pipeline from GS-15-4 would bring the combined gas to the onshore gas terminal at Odalarevu.

There was great suspense in finalizing the terminal. There was political pressure to locate the terminal on the other side of the river Odalarevu. But with determined effort and technical justification that, if the pipeline from offshore to the other side of landfall was considered, it would have passed through the river mouth and have the potential hazard of rupture during flooding of the river. With this justification the political pressure was defeated and Odalarevu terminal was finalized and land acquisition process initiated. In all this process, meeting external agencies and meeting the senior level executives of Rajahmundry project, I had to represent the E & C division though I was in a middle level. I was fortunate that whomever I had interacted with, everyone was positive and supportive. Mr. E. Venugopal, Chief Engineer, joined me later to help us overcome the obstacles in bringing out this development with his vast experience in handling projects. I had similar association with him for Heera field development at Bombay.

Some of the innovations that went into the project other than monopile and self-burial were: constructing bare minimum facilities (fit for purpose) on topside deck, one well drilling provision through monopile through a hatch arrangement on helideck, pile driving by hydraulic hammer thereby cutting cost of mobilizing a larger derrick barge with steam hammer facilities, fitting riser clamps onto monopile by Kevlar straps instead of conventional larger clamps to be fabricated in yard and installed offshore and adding the scope of work of certification services of the project to the contractor instead of separately engaging a certification agency etc.

6.4   New Concept for Burial of Offshore Pipelines

Burial of offshore subsea pipelines was for the safety & stability of the pipeline on the seabed. Generally, after laying the pipeline on seabed, a trenching machine or jet sled is lowered from a burial barge over the pipeline and trenching or jetting is carried out so that the pipeline moves into the trench formed and the pipeline gets buried fully in due course. The pipeline is buried to a depth of 1 meter cover which is later confirmed by a side scan survey measurement.

For a small project like GS-15/23 where there are only 2 small pipelines, the mobilization and demobilization costs of a jet barge/ burial barge would be very expensive compared to the actual duration of burial work at site. Also, this cost would impact the project economics towards unviability for a marginal oil field. offshore.

Fortunately, GS-15/23 area in KG-offshore was having soft soil conditions leading to self-burial of the pipelines by its own weight, cutting into the seabed. atleast up to the entire pipelines' diameter (flush buried). This was established by the survey conducted by M/S ESSAR for Ravva pipelines which was adjacent to GS-15/23 field.

Hence, "self-burial of pipelines was developed as a design concept. Though no paper or article was published by me on this, this worked well and was followed in other projects of the west coast later on. The concrete weight coating on the pipelines was increased in such a way that the negative buoyancy or weight in water of the pipeline was compensated enabling the pipeline to cut into the mud and get buried to flush level. The stability of the pipeline was designed with this extra concrete weight and flush buried condition. Though EIL, the designer of the pipeline was reluctant to consider the concept initially in the absence of any precedence, after persuasion and insistence and after their internal study, agreed to incorporate the design concept in the tender which was also later agreed by the bidders in the tender. The successful contractor M/S Clough Offshore, Australia, also proved its viability during detailed engineering stage and finally implemented it successfully.

Self-burial of pipelines was evolved by defining a design criteria for pipeline stability during installation with a 5-year storm criteria and pipeline stability during operation under a 50-year storm criteria with pipeline self-burial at least to flush buried condition. Also, the concrete coating on the pipeline was evolved for the pipeline to get self-

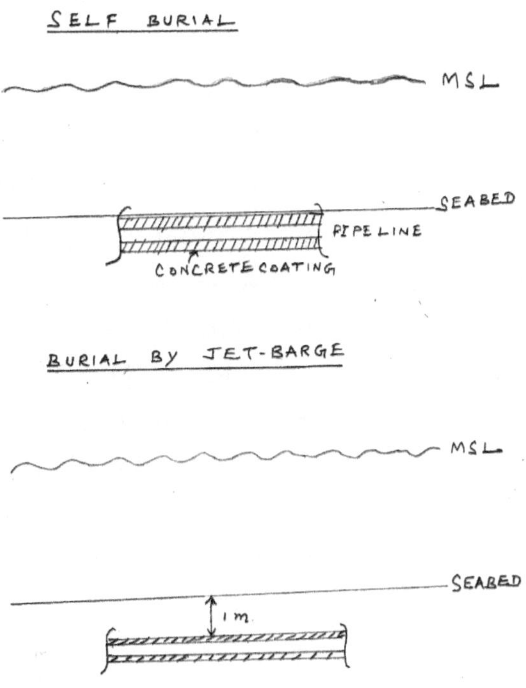

buried (i.e.,) extra weight coating was added more than required for laying. Generally concrete coating on the steel pipe is done to obtain negative buoyancy required for pipe laying.

The survey conducted later revealed that self-burial was achieved as per design philosophy and even at most places buried to more depth than the anticipated burial depth. The stability of the pipeline was thus established. This concept was later adopted in some projects of ONGC on the West Coast also, leading to considerable cost savings. Though, whether this concept is practiced elsewhere is not known, but this is a proven concept and can be applied where subsea soil conditions are conducive for self-burial.

6.5   Challenges in Monopile Design

For the monopile design the soil data was available only for 49m which was obtained for rig penetration calculations. Carrying out soil investigations by mobilizing a soil investigation vessel was not cost effective. Alternatively, it was proposed to use the same conservative soil data at the 30-49m strata up to the final depth of pile penetration required to support the platforms at GS-15/23 locations. The design of the monopiles were also done with careful overdrive allowance and confirm the adequacy of the monopile platform during driving of the pile by blow counts correlated to pile capacity. Ultimately the monopiles were designed as 94 and 96 inches for GS-15-4 & GS-23-1 locations. This was a great challenge technically, taking a calculated risk but with abuadant precautions (without full soil data) and that yielded a considerable cost saving to the project towards making the scheme techno-commercially viable.

Every other innovation mentioned above have contributed to cost saving thereby making GS-15/23 project one of the most economical offshore projects in the world and the first of its kind in Indian waters. Two monopile platforms and two pipelines came at a cost of just US $11.7 MM in 1999. CMD, ONGC gave an award to me as "Professional of the year" for making this project commercially viable with innovative design concepts.

It is pertinent to mention that this marginal field could not be developed for about 15 years after discovery due to non-viability by conventional platforms and known concepts.

Thanks are also due to the reservoir group which gave support by reworking the production profiles indicating condensate recovery which boosted the revenue for economic viability of the project. Late Shri.G.R.K. Murthy, GM (R) supported with full enthusiasm to ensure that this field was put on production.

IEOT/IOGPT also supported the project with the innovative concepts. Shri.B.D.Malhotra, Director IOGPT took special interest in making the project successful. Shri.C.P.Saha, the Regional Director at Chennai, whole heartedly supported the project and endorsed all the innovations to the ONGC board so that the board cleared the project for implementation.

However, there was a query from a member of the finance ministry that with too many innovations and risks, how could ONGC be confident to complete the project successfully. It was carefully explained one by one that all were independent items and none of them could lead to failure, the worst-case scenario could be a small cost increase which would not affect the viability. The Board cleared the sanction of the project with best wishes.

The basic design was given to EIL on modular basis with an intention to limit their role and cost to the project. It was decided that ONGC engineers would review/ inspect/supervise the detailed engineering, fabrication and installation works. Certification agency scope was already included in the contractor's scope with a condition that he should engage one of the reputed certification agencies as listed in the bid package.

The project was tendered through ICB and M/S Clough Offshore, Perth, Australia came out as the successful bidder. Mr. Kulasegaram Siritharan, the project manager assigned by M/S Clough, successfully executed the project in India for the first time within the schedule with no cost over-run.

The design review was held at Perth, Australia. I was stationed in Perth for a month to co-ordinate the design review along with civil, electrical and process discipline of ONGC engineers. Some of the technical issues which cropped up during detailed engineering of this innovative project and how they were resolved are worth mentioning. These were not visualized in the basic preparation of bid package.

One issue brought out was that as the platform was to be on a monopile and the deck was to be installed over the monopile through a single stabbing cone, getting the levels of the four corners of the deck within allowable limits was technically cumbersome as no level adjustment was possible during offshore installation which was feasible in 4-point mating. It was decided after discussion to include a new structure called "cruciform" which would consist of a central pin to be stabbed onto the monopile and four arms spread with four slots for taking the deck into it with four-point stabbing and installation and the platform deck would be integrated with it. It was pursued and agreed that this would not be treated as a change order by the contractor and the company would pay for the additional structural tonnage adjustment of the deck structure as provided in the contract. Shri. T.S.Rengarajan from IEOT reviewed the structural design.

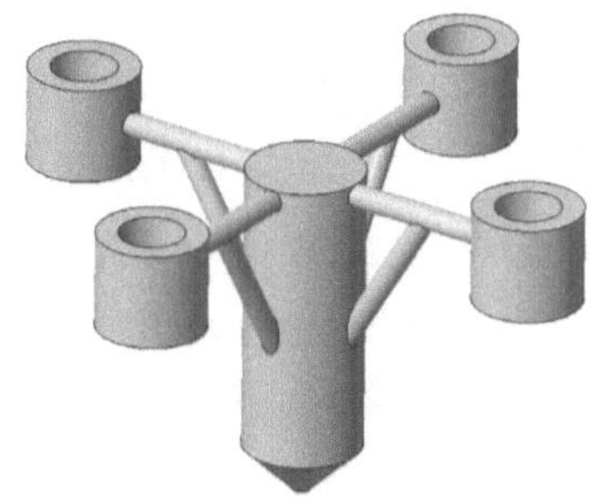

Another issue which was brought out, was the installation of the riser clamp supports onto the monopile at offshore by divers and its complexity and time involved in the works. One solution that was very innovative but not a well-established technology, though, and successfully performing for about 5 years in the Gulf of Mexico, was suggested by M/S Clough. As the design life of this platform was only 10 years and based on the strength of the robust technology, it was agreed to incorporate Kevlar Straps to hold the half clamps onto the monopile instead of conventional clamping arrangement. Here again, though the Kevlar was expensive the contractor agreed to forego the extra cost considering the time saved in the divers' work. The company also benefitted by not paying for the heavy clamps as per conventional method and only had to pay for the smallest structure weight. This was a win-win situation and resolved without reference to higher levels, tender committees etc., This resolution is not possible in today's ONGC. Similarly, the innovations of this project will not pass through in today's systems and procedures; hence, the bottle neck in the development of marginal fields with innovations, in my opinion.

A few other simple technical issues were also resolved then and there so that the detailed engineering was completed very fast, leading to commencement of fabrication earlier than schedule(d). The monopiles came out to be 94 and 96 inches Dia with about 70m penetration for GS-15/4 and GS-23-1 locations. Against a conventional platform tonnage of 1000 to 1200T for these locations it came out to be just around 320 Tonnes only which is a huge saving thereby for commercial viability of this field. Apart from the low cost of the project, the schedule achieved was also very short (i.e.) 6 ½ months from LOI.

It is pertinent to note that these platforms and pipelines served their design life successfully and even survived the Tsunami in 2015.

6.6   Plan for G-1/GS-15 Development

GS-15/23 project is the fore runner for ONGC's Eastern offshore asset at Kakinada, now established as a larger asset. During conception, finalization, and implementation of GS-15/23 project, I also conceptualized further development of GS-15 and G-1 fields, in modular concept. Further, I also visualized that more modern technologies would evolve for deep water developments with more economical concepts in future and hence it would be prudent to develop G-1 field integrated with GS-15 development in a phased manner. One such concept evolved by me was to install a monopile oil platform for location GS-15-1 and produce oil from GS-15-1 and GS-15-4 as a module, subsequently subsea wells of G-1 could be supported from GS-15-1 or at a nearby new shallow water platform. Power could be sent to this platform from land terminal to offshore for supporting the subsea wells and controls. The well fluid so produced could be transported to Odalarevu terminal for processing. All these developments should be done only on a modular basis to avoid huge losses as the risk involved in the reserves and G-1 field is high. During conceptual studies I even assumed that future water injection systems could be made as modular at subsea location as new technologies may mature by that time and only power cables are to be laid to the location, instead of processing through a central water injection facility and distributing this through pipeline networks. Pipeline networks could be replaced with power cable networks and subsea water injection modules with considerable energy and cost savings.

Modular concepts in the cost range of a few hundred cores at a time was planned to mitigate the risk involved in G-1 and deep-water developments, adjacent to GS-15 field.

It is very unfortunate that ONGC completely changed the concept evolved by me after transferring me to the Eastern Region, Jorhat. For ONGC, transferring a person to Eastern Region is more important than the benefits of not transferring a suitable experienced person in the ongoing offshore development. The general policy of job rotation and catering to the requirements of Eastern region was affecting the expertise build up and benefits to the company and exodus of expertise, which was never studied by HR and the transfers were implemented on a one to one basis. It is based on

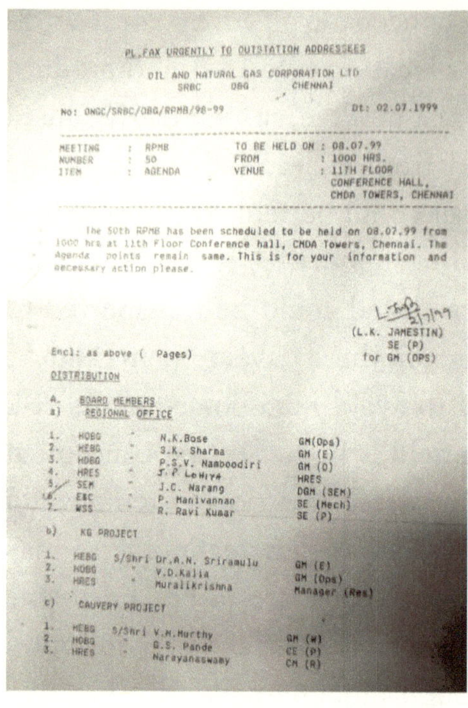

discipline, that is a mechanical engineer who gained expertise in one area would be sent to a completely new area without any justification even compromising the project requirements, which is very sad.

By strict implementation of my transfer to the Eastern Region and transfer of a few others in E&C division, Chennai, the division became very weak and finally the section was closed. Also, further development of the East Coast was taken up by Mumbai E & C division, which was later transferred to Eastern offshore asset, Kakinada. This transition led to the scrapping of all the concepts evolved for GS-15/G-1 development by E & C division Chennai, on modular concept and a completely new strategy of development was evolved. A single mega project was conceived which later turned out to be a misadventure and ultimately approx. Rs. 4000crs was sunk with very poor/meager return on investment. Even large compressors were procured as part of mega project, unused, and kept idle for long. In the scheme originally conceived by E & C division, Chennai, these were to be procured later after a few years of production. Initially, only the hiring of compressors of smaller capacity was envisaged.

This proves why experience and the right strategy in planning offshore development is essential. This example and JV methodology of exploitation of PY-3 put together lost thousands of crores by not following the right strategy and ignoring the experience and expertise of its own engineers.

6.7 Plan for GS-29 Field

During those times before leaving the E & C division, I also evolved a strategy for GS-29 field development in the East Coast. GS-29-1 is an oil bearing well and could not be monetized for a long time due to commercial non-viability as the water depth at GS-29-1 is 120m.

I conceived an imaginary scheme for development of GS-29-1 in which a similarly producing well in shallow water if proved to be oil bearing nearby to this location was developed. By discussion with EBG an exploratory well GS-29-AB at 10m water depth was identified for exploratory drilling on priority so that if this proved to be oil bearing, a platform could be installed in the shallow water and at GS-29-1 a subsea well could be completed to transport oil by pipeline to the land fall point through this platform. An imaginary feasibility report was prepared which was found to be economically viable. RPMB meetings held with other discipline heads for early production of fields supported the idea. The success of implementation of GS-15/23 also was similar with multi-disciplinary approach. I presented a poster in one of the conferences held at Baroda about the success story of GS-15/23 and Southern Region's future plans with same approach for other marginal fields. I am not sure if this approach is existing in the present Asset and Basins concept to augment production of hydrocarbons.

The Regional Director, as noted above, advised drilling the exploratory well GS-29-AB on priority. But this exploratory well turned out to be dry as officially reported. However, I still have doubts about the result, as I heard there were drilling complications which could have led to the wrong result. The rig was a hired rig. It is a pity that this development is still pending even after more than 20 years. The synergy of production in parallel with exploration, the concept practiced during the days of regional directors, is now dead in ONGC.

Dr. Col.S.P. Wahi in his book "Leading from the front" had written about GS-15/23 that "It is a pity that GS-15/23 development has happened only after 15 years of discovery" for which my innovations came to rescue. But who will rescue GS-29 development is to be seen?

When GS-15/23 was about to be commissioned, I was summoned to go on transfer to Eastern Region. As my efforts for retention to continue with offshore development on the East Coast did not yield any result, I decided to move to NIOT, as a Scientist-F as that opportunity came as

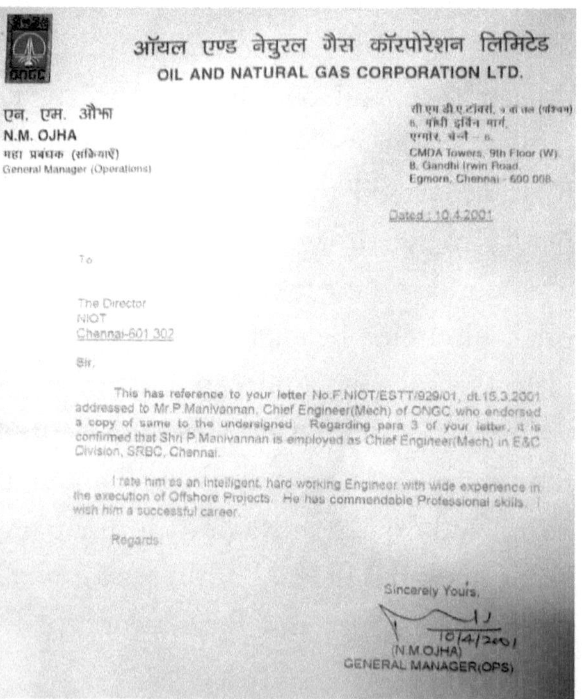

ऑयल एण्ड नेचुरल गैस कॉर्पोरेशन लिमिटेड
OIL AND NATURAL GAS CORPORATION LTD.

एन. एम. औझा
N.M. OJHA
महा प्रबंधक (संक्रियाएँ)
General Manager (Operations)

सी.एम.डी.ए.टावर्स, ९ वां तल (पश्चिम)
८, गांधी इर्विन मार्ग,
एग्मोर, चेन्नई - ८.
CMDA Towers, 9th Floor (W).
8, Gandhi Irwin Road.
Egmore, Chennai - 600 008.

Dated : 10.4.2001

To

The Director
NIOT
Chennai-601 302

Sir,

This has reference to your letter No.F.NIOT/ESTT/929/01, dt.15.3.2001 addressed to Mr.P.Manivannan, Chief Engineer(Mech) of ONGC who endorsed a copy of same to the undersigned. Regarding para 3 of your letter, it is confirmed that Shri P.Manivannan is employed as Chief Engineer(Mech) in E&C Division, SRBC, Chennai.

I rate him as an intelligent, hard working Engineer with wide experience in the execution of Offshore Projects. He has commendable Professional skills. I wish him a successful career.

Regards.

Sincerely Yours,

10/4/2001
(N.M.OJHA)
GENERAL MANAGER(OPS)

a blessing in disguise. I also felt that as anyway ONGC was not going to use my experience or expertise in offshore anymore and I had to move to another area of work, at least I could serve for some more years in the ocean engineering field. I was selected by the Department of Ocean Development (DOD), now Ministry of Earth Sciences, as scientist-F to take up the Mission of the World's first 1MW Ocean Thermal Energy Conversion project (OTEC) demonstration. As the position as a senior scientist was a quantum jump in level, and interesting, I agreed to take up the assignment on deputation as I wanted to come back to ONGC, anyway. The DOD needed an experienced offshore person to head the OTEC project for implementation off-Tuticorin port in South India. There were negative comments from senior colleagues from ONGC, that I was moving on to work with a lower salary, though true, it was a senior position equivalent to Joint secretary in ministry. Prof. M.Ravindran was kind to add three increments in my pay scale to adjust the salary loss to some extent.

* * *

Chapter 7

Deputation to NIOT for OTEC project

After joining NIOT in 2001, I was heading the OTEC mission mode project, till 2004. Immediately after joining NIOT, I moved to Tuticorin to oversee the arrangements in Tuticorin Port for welding HDPE pipes in Harbor area, pre-commissioning of facilities on OTEC barge which arrived at Tuticorin Port from Dempo Shipyard, Goa after construction. The OTEC barge

was constructed already before my joining. I got the guidance and support from Dr. Jayamani, who retired from ISRO (GSLV project) and was associated as advisor to the OTEC project in addition to the guidance and directions from prof. M. Ravindran, founder Director of NIOT. Other senior scientists of NIOT also supported the implementation of the OTEC project as this was the most important project of NIOT at that time.

Ocean Thermal Energy Conversion is a process of producing electricity by utilizing the heat source of warm water on the sea surface and the heat sink of cold water at 1000m deep in the ocean. A closed cycle, liquid vapour, ammonia system installed on the OTEC barge does this job. Liquid ammonia is evaporated in a heat exchanger by warm surface water. The vapour generated by this process turns the turbine to generate electricity. The energy-exhausted vapour is then cooled by the cold water drawn by 1km long HDPE pipe from the sea-bottom in another heat exchanger to condense the vapour back into liquid ammonia. This process was done in a closed cycle, thereby continuously producing electricity. I don't intend to go deeper into the technical aspects.

I made two major observations on the system already conceived by my predecessors associated with the OTEC project. One was keeping the cold-water pipe which brought cold water from deep sea as part of single point mooring system of the OTEC barge at the location of power production. I had my own doubts about this already conceived arrangement and all configurations were finalized accordingly. Another one was keeping the living quarters on OTEC barge at the opposite end of the mooring bollard. In case of an ammonia leak from the system during the operation, the gas would enter the living area due to wind blowing towards the living quarters from the barge's bow end to the aft end in a single point mooring configuration.

As the project was only for demonstration and not for the long time running of the plant as a commercial facility, I had to agree with the inputs already gone into the project and proceeded with the same. A few other arrangements were also of some minor concern but could not be revised at that stage.

7.1 Drilling Difficulty in GS-15/23 Resolved

Within a month of my joining NIOT there was an urgent call from ONGC that the innovative platforms we designed for GS-15/23 were not suitable for the drilling rig to re-enter and complete the exploratory wells as the conductor guides were not in line and not concentric to the well alignment. Rig Sagar Ratna was on standby mode for about 10 days. A lot of mudslinging was done on me personally and on the E & C division, Chennai by the drilling department. Later, after my visit to the site on the drilling rig, it was proved that it was a silly issue and could have been solved by them with some common sense.

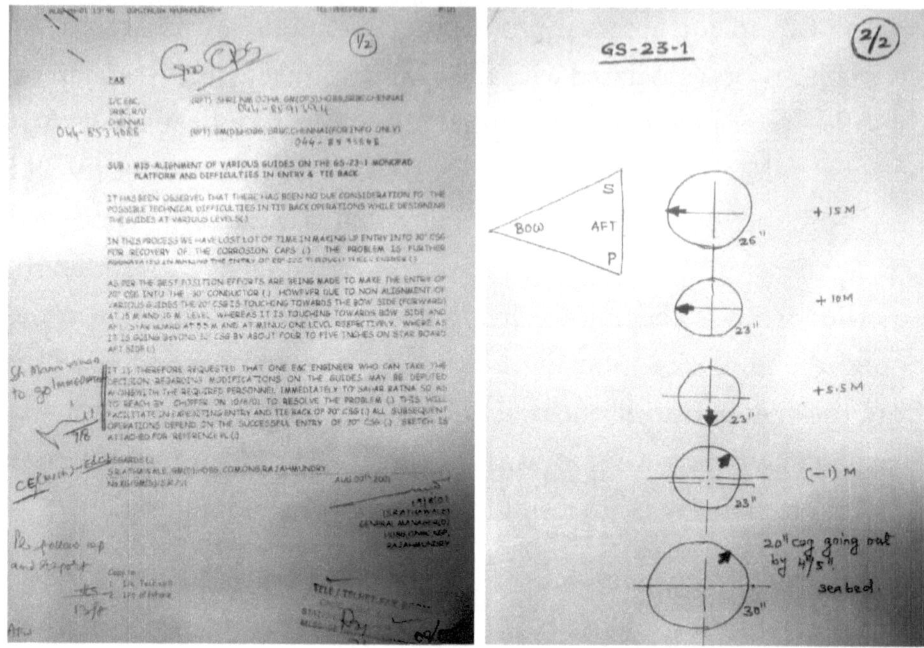

I rushed to the drilling rig with another ONGC colleague Shri. Ajay Kumar Singh and studied the problem. I asked them to fabricate a funnel and inserted it onto the exploratory well head top. Now I asked the drilling rig to insert the conductor from the rig through the guide and finally guided by the funnel. It went inside perfectly and fitted. After that the funnel was cut & removed by the divers. The well was later completed successfully, I came out of criticism and I am thankful to Shri.S.R.Athawale, then GM(Drilling) for his kind acceptance and directions to his drilling team in implementing my suggestions towards successful solution to the problem. GS-15/23 was successfully commissioned later. Though this was innovated, conceived, and successfully implemented, I could not be present for the successful commissioning and the inaugural functions related to the same, as I was with NIOT on deputation.

This is not the only time I missed seeing the successful finale and witnessing the celebrations, there were many other cases during my career with ONGC/NIOT.

I think I should at least list them in brief for the reader to note that such things are normal in a government servant's career.

One is the development of HeeraPh-II development. After doing all the spade work and got the development sanctioned, I had to move out of Mumbai to Chennai, due to unexpected turn outs (E & C shuffles) and other circumstances. It was only news to me that this field developed into a major oil field with the innovative ideas and schemes evolved during our combined efforts with Shri.E. Venugopal sir.

Another one is the PATENT and new construction technique developed during my Mumbai, E & C tenure which never came to light, as I could not be present there to follow up and implement, though a paper was published in ISOPE-91, and available to read through Google search. Another project was Ravva Phase-II, this was not only for me, for many ONGCians as it was privatized by Government policy.

Another one was on my return to ONGC from NIOT after 3 years of deputation, due to CMD, ONGC's denial for 2 years extension as requested by secretary, DOD, Government of India. I could not be present in NIOT during the successful demonstration of offshore OTEC desalination with the OTEC barge off-Chennai by independently mooring the OTEC barge on single point mooring with wire rope and separately holding the HDPE cold water pipe hanging from the barge from a central moon pool. This was the concept I thought viable when I joined NIOT, which was successfully done by Dr. S.Kathiroli, the next director of NIOT. Also, I could not visit Kavaratti Island even once for the first LLTD plant, which was commissioned in 2005, though I was involved in the conceptual plan of offshore facilities and further, the use of minimum marine facilities in that remote island to construct economically, were planned during my tenure with NIOT. My experience in offshore jackets fabrication, load out and installation methods were applied for economic benefits for the island conditions along-with other participants in the various meetings chaired by Prof. M Ravindran.

However, I visited Lakshadweep Island for review of additional LTTD plants sanctioned by Government of India in 6 more islands as a TCEC committee member later, after my retirement from ONGC in Feb 2020. It was a pleasant feeling that the simple offshore conceptualization for Kavaratti plant (1st one) is being repeatedly used in all the islands for supplying fresh water to the island communities. A total of 9 plants have been sanctioned by the Government for the island communities for their safe drinking water.

One another project that saw light was the Borholla to Khoraghat trunk pipeline of 65 km length after my joining Engineering Services in 2005, at Jorhat. As I had to leave Jorhat in 2008 after completion of my tenure in North-East and the pipeline could be commissioned only in 2012-13 due to obstacles by local vested interests of the tanker lobby(?) which was interested in transportation of the crude by road. This pipeline was commissioned as a prestigious project of the Assam asset, ONGC, with the presence of CMD and senior officers of ONGC.

Now returning to my journey, I continued with NIOT till 2004, and implemented the activities of OTEC. The necessary documentation for sanction by the Government for deployment and other related expenditure was prepared and submitted to the ministry, as we(myself), Dr. Jayamani and Prof. Ravindran camped in Delhi to get the proposal cleared. Dr. H.K. Gupta, secretary, and Dr. S.Y. Quraishi, additional secretary, was appraised of the proposal. Dr. Quraishi, IAS officer (later became 17th CEC of India) was also keen in listening to the OTEC principle and understanding of the research, and Prof. Ravindran introduced me to him as Chief Engineer, from ONGC, and about my experience in offshore installations. Dr. Quraishi supported the proposal with his other IAS counterparts for the timely clearance of the expenditure sanction.

7.2 Pre-commissioning Activities-OTEC Barge

All pre-commissioning activities on OTEC barge were carried out at Tuticorin Port and a few km away in shallow water. Running the cold and warm water pumps, storage, and maintenance of ammonia on OTEC barge, observation of OTEC barge on single point mooring in sea at shallow water etc., were demonstrated successfully. Dr. Jayamani Sir's association in the pre-commissioning activities were a new kind of experience which was different from ONGC, where the combined procedures of ONGC and ISRO style were implemented and demonstrated to show the successful functioning of the plant. Shri Vedachalam and Shri Palaniappan and few other devoted scientists posted at Tuticorin, assisted in the pre-commisioning activities. Shri.Raju Abraham from the Chennai office also visited most of the time for the activities at Tuticorin and sea trials. The power plant, evaporating ammonia and running the turbine generator on no-load and part load (Lights) was successfully demonstrated. The ammonia vapour from the turbine was let out as it could not be cooled with cold water unless we went to a deep-water location. The only pending demonstrations left, were the successful deployment of the cold-water pipe and mooring system in deep water and successful withdrawal (pumping) of cold water from deep sea for feeding into OTEC barge at location on mooring and continuous production of OTEC power. These were planned for final demonstration.

During pre-commissioning activities of OTEC barge an air-conditioning system based on cold water was also incorporated in the barge for air-conditioning the control rooms. This was also tested successfully using ice cubes procured locally at an ice factory in Tuticorin. The Scheme was submitted with my initiative to PCRA(Petroleum Conservation Research Association) in 2003. We deputed a scientist Shri Narayanan to New Delhi to receive the award. An award was given to NIOT by PCRA for the cold water-based air conditioning as a by-product of OTEC. Another by-product is OTEC desalination which is also called LTTD (Low Temperature Thermal Desalination) which was successfully implemented in Lakshadweep islands. Airconditioning is also a potential byproduct.

The cold-water pipe (HDPE) was welded in Tuticorin Port and sub-assemblies of fabricated components of mooring system were organized to be ready for deployment 40km off Tuticorin Port.

7.3 Final Deployment -off Tuticorin

A tender was floated for selection of a deployment contractor whose scope of work was to assemble the components at Port, tow the assembled pipe and mooring system to site and deploy the system at site. I incorporated certain clauses, terms & conditions from ONGC offshore contract relevant to this tender. The work was awarded to M/s Madgaonkar, Goa and they mobilized the barge 'Himmat' for the deployment operations. Meetings were held at Goa, Chennai and Tuticorin to review the sequence of activities, deployment procedures and safety aspects including co-ordination with various agencies. Experts were involved in review and their comments were taken note of and incorporated. A HAZID study was also taken up by a foreign expert towards safety of the system during tow and deployment, at my insistence as followed in critical offshore installations.

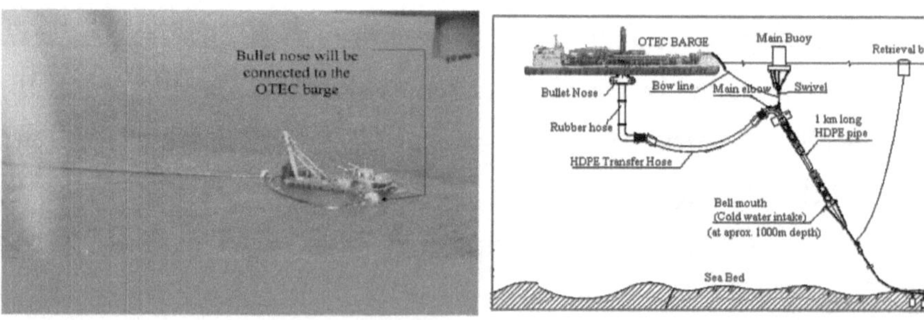

M/s Madgaonkar mobilized their marine spread to Tuticorin, and the assembly works were carried out at Tuticorin Port. After the assembly, the pipe and mooring system were towed to a location with clear weather window for tow and deployment.

Though the deployment of the mooring system was successful along with the 1km long cold-water pipe, as the transfer hose got snapped from the main pipe, further operations could not be taken up. Attempts were made to connect the transfer hose but in vain. Also due to continuous heavy heaving of the surface buoy, chafing of the chain elements led to snapping of the surface buoy and it drifted away. The pipe and mooring system sunk to the bottom. Efforts and plans to retrieve the system failed and further attempts were stopped due to the prohibitory cost of the recovery process in deep water.

Dr. Jayamani and I visited a Singapore based deep water salvaging company for the recovery process and to explain to them the installation process and components sunk at a location of around 1000m water depth. The quote given by the company was almost the same as the cost of the system lost.

Further, I personally felt at that time, if the concept of keeping the cold-water pipe as part of mooring system was eliminated and a separate independent mooring system was planned, though at a cost, this fate would not have probably occurred, as mooring and cold-water withdrawal, the two separate functions, would be isolated. Though the Orcaflex software analysis showed satisfactory results as projected, I had my reservations and as opined by me, OTEC desalination was successfully proved with the same OTEC barge off Chennai Port subsequently, with an independent wire rope single point mooring system by attaching the cold-water pipe separately to the barge. Also, I felt one of the major constraints in Ocean research is the disproportionately meagre budgets and facilities provided for a highly challenging research activity leading to compromise and cost cutting. In my opinion, cost cutting should be applied to commercial projects, not to research as the concentration should be on the principle to be demonstrated, not on economizing on infrastructure for the demonstration.

I was informed by Prof. Ravindran that initially NIOT tried to acquire Sagar Prabhat(ONGCs floater Rig) for OTEC, which was planned to be scrapped due to its drilling equipment aging. The scrap cost of Sagar Prabhat also could not be accommodated within the budget allotted for OTEC demonstration. I felt either an arrangement between ministries for use of the platform for few years till the demonstration or any other mode of ensuring the use of this giant vessel, could have helped to draw the cold water from 1000m with easy mooring at this depth leading to complete the final task seamlessly. It was all too late to realize, but I could not keep this buried in my mind, when we failed to draw cold sea water from 1000m off Tuticorin to conclude the 1 MW, OTEC plant demonstration.

As I mentioned earlier, as the shallow water trials proved the concept except for the quantification of net power that could be derived from the 1MW plant, required for future extrapolation for larger plants in the sea, towards commercialization. In the larger interest of India, I hope being a well placed tropical country, OTEC could become a continuous source of power in future, and this may be realized sooner or later and Prof. M.Ravindran's dream could see the light, as many new technologies on OTEC power extraction with improvements in efficiency on evaporation, condensation, improvements in structures and ease of deployment etc. One can refer to the latest Patents being filed on OTEC even till recently.

7.4 Conference Papers

During my deputation with NIOT, few international and national level conference papers were written by me and these were well received by the scientific community. One of the papers referred to by international scientists on OTEC is the international conference paper "OTEC Economics, the perception, and the future" which can be searched in Google. In this paper, a comparison was made with OTEC and a marginal offshore oil field to show its feasibility to commercialize OTEC soon. I have included a paper submitted to Petrotech - 2016 for the reference of readers which covers various options and the potential of OTEC as a future energy source with minimal environmental concerns.

Another interesting work done during my stay with NIOT was exploring offshore wind energy options for India. I made lecture notes and presented to SAARC country delegates at Chennai, organized by C-WET, Chennai on offshore wind energy. This impetus continued in NIOT for various foundation options and economic studies on offshore wind energy to suit Indian waters, and I witnessed and contributed to the discussions as part of the Scientific advisory council of NIOT. It's a pity that offshore wind energy is yet to take off in India and I understand that the

Government of India is taking steps towards offshore wind energy installations in the East coast and West coast.

Another major milestone for OTEC in India was to write a project report titled "Pre-feasibility studies for OTEC commercialization in India". This study was sponsored by NTPC, a premier power producing company in India. This work was the first of its kind in India giving a road map for OTEC in India. Only very few road maps on OTEC are available even as of date worldwide. This is a good reference document even today for the OTEC group and OTEC enthusiasts in India. NTPC appreciated the work; however, they could not enter into a commercial arrangement to put up a land based small OTEC pre-commercial plant in Kavaratti Island as the first step towards commercialization as proposed in the report. Another large scale plant at Cheyyur in Tamil Nadu coast was also recommended as another candidate for a commercial OTEC plant. Dr. Raju Abraham and few other scientists at design office contributed in bringing out this report which could serve as a guide for future.(Refer Annexure for some details).

Another great chance missed by me was to present OTEC technology to our late president Dr. A.P.J. Abdul Kalam and take his guidance and blessing for OTEC demonstration and advancement in India as a pioneer country. Dr. Jayamani Sir, who was an advisor to OTEC, suggested that one day we could go to the College of Engineering, Guindy and meet Dr. Kalam who was a Chair Professor and stayed there at Guindy, to invite him as he was his close associate in ISRO, to take his guidance and blessings. But unfortunately for us, and fortunately for the country he was invited to Delhi to become president in 2002 and became inaccessible to us, during our project implementation. Later, I had known his interest in oil and gas development and his interactions with Col. S.P. Wahi, former CMD, ONGC and the missing of this visit to NIOT for OTEC briefing was felt by me for long.

On the sidelines of OTEC power project, OTEC desalination technology was also parallelly planned for implementation. A potential site at Kavaratti Island was chosen for OTEC desalination. In OTEC desalination, the warm surface water is flash evaporated in a vacuum chamber and the resultant vapour is then cooled by the cold water drawn from 800-1000m depth of the ocean. As the topography of Lakshadweep islands is that a drop of 800 to 1000m of the ocean depth, takes place adjacent to the landfall point, it was easy to bring the cold water through HDPE pipe laid into the dropping topography of the island. The contour of the coast in the island is such that the shallow water extends to few hundred meters from the coastline to a depth 5-10m and then drops to a deep trench. These islands are like the top of hills in the deep ocean. Various options were studied and conceptualized for the drawl of cold and warm waters for the OTEC desalination. One lakh litres per day capacity was planned as a pilot project at Kavaratti (an island in the union territory of Lakshadweep, India which is in the Arabian sea). This project was coordinated by another senior scientist Dr. Robert Singh who was on deputation like me to NIOT from DRDO, Hyderabad.

Various options for economical installation of facilities were discussed by Prof. Ravindran, Dr. S. Kathiroli, few IIT Professors and a simple economical and easy to execute methodology in a remote island was evolved. The concept of having a trestle and open jetty in the sea for Ravva Phase-II project, was explored as an option for exporting crude through oil tankers, various methods of load out of jackets and offshore facilities, pipeline laying methods, shore-pull done for GS-15/23 were some of the inputs put-forth by me, some of which have gone into the scheme for implementation with minimum marine infrastructure.

An open trestle up to 5m water depth was to be laid and at 5m depth the sump for drawl of cold-water was proposed to be erected. This sump would be connected to the cold-water pipe which would draw the cold water. Both cold & warm water pumps will be installed above the sump and the power line, pipelines and walkways run through the trestle. These conceptual designs were also included in our report to NTPC on prefeasibility studies for OTEC power plant at an island location.

This configuration was finalized and implemented successfully as a pilot project. Based on the success of this pilot project more LTTD desalination plants were being built and operated for the

island community drinking water needs.

This pilot project was commissioned after I left NIOT and returned back to ONGC.

Further, considering the remoteness of the islands and non-availability of marine spread, simple methods of prefabricating structural components, tow and erection were evolved considering minimum handling equipment. The sump was planned to be prefabricated at the lagoon side of the island and launched into water by pushing with hydraulic Jacks into the water and towing to the other side where it was to be positioned. Also, the plant components were planned to be moved by trolleys/tractors and with chain pulley block arrangements lifted and erected with innovative ideas. This helped in economizing the project cost without mobilizing larger marine equipment to the remote island. Same concepts are being followed for building additional desalination plants on these islands. For interested readers a video, made by NIOT later is available in you-tube to know more about the various methodologies for construction and HDPE pipe deployment.

When we were left with the failure of the cold-water pipe & mooring in the floating OTEC plant system, various ideas were conceptualized. One of the ideas that was put forth by me was instead of bringing the cold water to the surface from deep sea, why not take the heat exchanger to the sea bottom and send the vapour down and bring it back as liquid. It was a great surprise to me that this idea was later found to be patented after a few years of my leaving NIOT. This I have referred in my paper submitted to Petrotech 2016.

Further I authored few technical papers on Ocean Thermal Energy Conversion and presented in national and international conferences during my tenure with NIOT and even later. In an international conference arranged by CBIP(Central Board of Irrigation and Power) at New Delhi, (2004), on the sidelines of the presentation on OTEC, during introduction, I shared my opinion that "Renewable energy was the only source of energy available for mankind till the past few hundred years, ever since the discovery of fossil fuels. Unfortunately, we call the renewable energy used by man since thousands of years as non-conventional energy which is a misnomer. Also we call the ministry dealing with renewable energy as MNES(Ministry of non-conventional energy) which needs correction. After the presentation of the paper, Secretary, CBIP, congratulated me and thanked me for my opinion and assured me that he would do the needful for the correction and to my surprise very soon the ministry was renamed MNRE(Ministry of new and renewable energy).

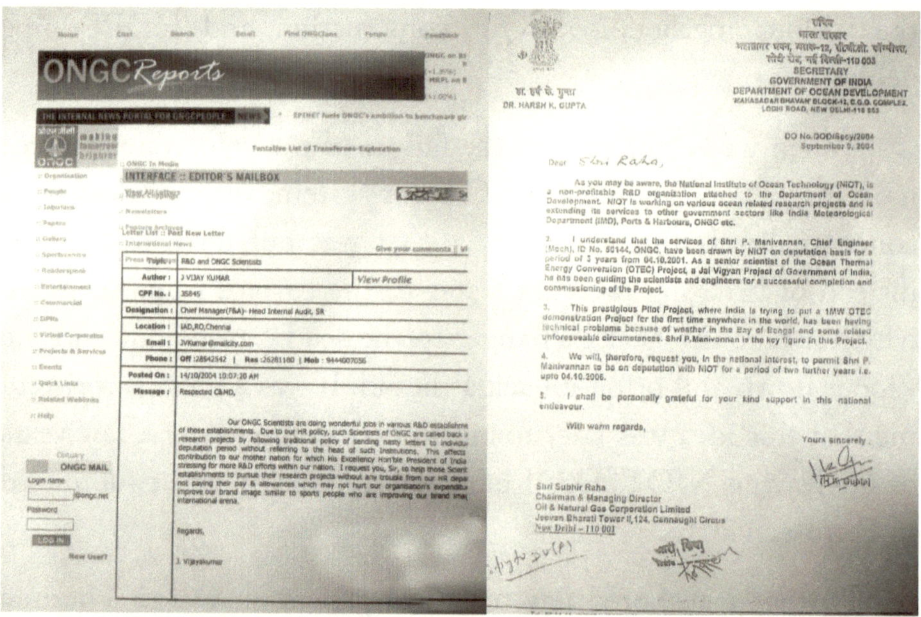

In Oct 2004, after I completed my deputation period in NIOT, I was advised to return to ONGC. As I was pursuing alternate methodologies for proving OTEC power generation in NIOT, the secretary, DOD sought an extension of my deputation with NIOT for at least 2 more years to lead the team. As the new CMD, ONGC did not agree to this, I had no other option but to rejoin ONGC abruptly leaving the OTEC program. Subsequently, it so happened that OTEC power demonstration was abandoned and only OTEC desalination was pursued. OTEC desalination was proved with the OTEC barge off Chennai Port. Also at Kavaratti land based OTEC desalination plant was successfully commissioned.

After a few years the OTEC barge was scrapped as the Government did not sanction funds for another attempt. Though I proposed taking the OTEC barge to Kavaratti islands and moor it nearby and draw cold/warm water in a safer condition, that could not be pursued after I left. Even today I am confident that OTEC closed cycle power generation could be proved successfully with proper infrastructure. It is a pity that the final OTEC power demonstration is still an incomplete dream due to the single failure of the cold-water withdrawal, which was purely an infrastructure issue and not due to any other issues. The great inputs of Prof. Ravindran and his close associates in developing many technologies like multistage axial flow turbine, manufactured indigenously, the efficacy of plate heat exchangers etc. could not see light and I still repent for it. Even now, I remember the explanation on black board by Prof. M. Ravindran, the development of multistage axial flow turbine, indigenously, and its efficacy for low pressure application with velocity triangles and direction of forces etc (as in class room teaching) and the pleasure when it was running smoothly during the pre-commissioning activities. The argument that we should follow developed nations with respect to OTEC research is a wrong notion considering our country's long coast line in the tropical region with huge OTEC resources. The strategy of space research is not fair to be applied to OTEC research or for that matter any Ocean technology research. The agony of the proponents of OTEC research in India needs to be weighed and reviewed for the benefit of our country and OTEC power generation to be revived with its potential byproducts.

As of now an OTEC powered desalination plant is planned in Kavaratti, with open cycle power generation and producing water simultaneously. In my opinion, this research is not very beneficial even if successfully completed as it cannot be scaled up for larger capacities due to unacceptable turbine diameters required for larger plants.

* * *

Chapter 8

Eastern Region, ONGC, ASSAM-Engg. Services, Johrat

After joining back ONGC at Chennai from where I was relieved, Chennai office advised me to proceed immediately to Jorhat in Assam to join A &AA basin. When I left ONGC it had the business groups concept, with Regions and Regional Directors. When I returned in 2004, the new CMD, Shri. SubirRaha transformed ONGC into Assets and Basins concept.

Personally, I believe this restructuring has done more harm than good with respect to oil production and effective utilisation of resources. Though reserve accretions have shown positive trends, the corresponding increase in production was not achieved. The earlier approach of multidisciplinary joint development plans parallelly during exploration phase was missing, which gave more confidence, to exploration as well as to production. Effective utilization of resources was hampered due to compartmentalization of assets and basins. The earlier

Regional Directors effectively used the resources towards better utilization and more production output which was found to be lacking in this restructuring, leading to delayed development and large investment failures. In my opinion this will only take ONGC downwards and no betterment will be achieved in terms of energy security. I stop with this humble opinion and will not pass any more comments on this.

Coming to my further journey at Jorhat in ONGC from Feb 2005 till May 2008, it was really a different life. Professionally there was no setback, however, I could have contributed much better to an offshore field development. Anyway, ONGC's policy of compulsory posting of everyone at Eastern Region cannot be violated which is more important for ONGC. This is how ONGC works, and no visible actions or policy change has been taken so far to effectively utilize expertise. Either experts leave the organizations to continue their passion with better prospects in international organizations or those who accept the change to become a generalist, having to perform at a lower level of expertise in another area, both are a big loss for ONGC. A different approach for grooming generalists with aspirations for senior managerial positions rather than expertise building, could be more suitable for an oil major, is my opinion.

8.1   Borolla - Khoraghat 65 KM Pipeline

In Jorhat, I was posted to onshore engineering services. One major benefit of my posting at Jorhat was the implementation of the Khoraghat to Borolla, 65km long crude transfer pipeline. This pipeline was conceived 10 years earlier but did not take off as no one was effectively projecting the economics of implementation of this pipeline or there was pressure not to pursue diligently. The oil produced at Khoraghat fields was transported through road tankers to Borolla and then transferred to a refinery. This involved huge cost of logistics on road tankers, maintaining the roads and frequent spending on such road repairs, loss of oil due to accidental spillage, evaporation etc. It was noted that the strong tanker lobby was also a reason for the pipeline project not taking off. I have noticed in the file on this pipeline, that the cost of the pipeline implementation was compared with the annual cost of road tankers only and no proper economic analysis was carried out. The payback period was coming out with an unacceptable figure and hence management was also not inclined to approve the project. The case file was moving up and down with no concrete decision to either go for it or discard it. I thought of rewriting the proposal with the economic viability analysis on IRR (Internal rate of return) method as done for major projects and followed in offshore field development viability analysis. With my experience in writing FR (Feasibility Report) for offshore projects, I considered the revenue from the project as the annual cost of road transfer by tankers plus annual cost of road repairs and maintenance incurred, plus cost of crude due to evaporation loss as addition. This way the project was found to be commercially viable, which was not projected in the earlier proposals. Further justification on the pipeline was that even after exploitation of the Khoraghat and other nearby fields, this pipeline could be converted into a product pumping pipeline to deliver petroleum products to that area, with these projected economic viability and prospects, the management approved the project, for implementation on top priority.

8.2   Challenges in Implementation of Trunk Pipeline

The next obstacle for implementation was tendering for the project from Jorhat office, as there was apprehension that no suitable bidder would come forward to submit a bid at Jorhat due to inherent deterrence from the tanker lobby. The tender document was prepared. I proposed to the Basin Manager Shri. J.S. Sekhon that it was wise to float the tender from Engineering services, Mumbai with support from onshore Engg. Services group at Baroda. Shri.Y.Bhatnagar ED, onshore Engg. Services Group supported the plan and the management also agreed to this methodology as a special case.

Shri.R.S.Khati, the then Suptg. Engineer and I had to frequently move to Baroda, Mumbai and successfully awarded the work to M/S AFCONS, Mumbai. This methodology successfully worked for the award of this large project. Later, the same concept was used for tendering and award of Mega projects of Assam assets like Assam renewal project etc.

After the award of the pipeline project, a kickoff meeting was held at Jorhat, a pre-engineering Survey by the contractor was coordinated and later the detailed engineering works were done at Mumbai and Bangalore. I had to move to Mumbai and Bangalore and camp for many days as no other experienced person for handling the engineering review from the project group was available. At this time my health deteriorated and I had to stay at Bangalore with my wife to take care of me during the stay. With all the difficulties, I completed the engineering review successfully. After this I had to take leave and stay at Chennai for treating my health problems.

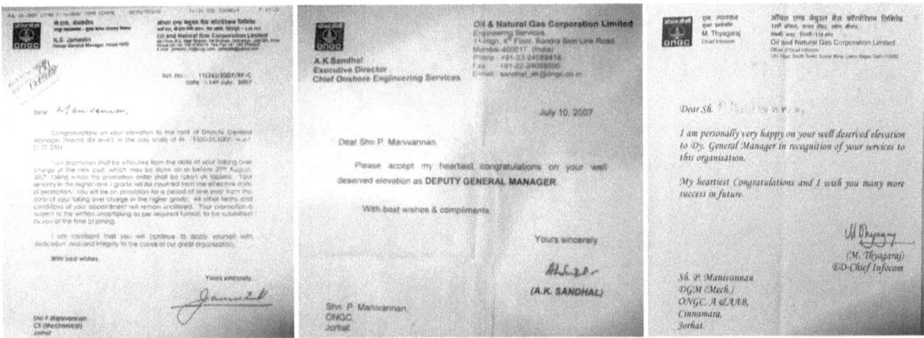

During this time a promotion order to the level of Dy.Gen, Manager was issued in favour of me. This was released in 2007 and the promotion was with effect from 1-1-2006. Due to health constraints, I could not join the new post for some time and could join only when the joining time was almost about to lapse. As soon as I joined the post, I was shifted to the Specialist Group at Jorhat as the seniority positions in the Engineering Services group of Jorhat was changing, and I should have become the Head Engg services. Considering my health condition, and to avoid embarrassment to the person already heading the engineering services, I was put in a specialist group by the local management. I had no regrets as this was a soft posting with less workload and helped me in treating my health condition by taking leave and visiting my hometown for treatment with family support. Though I was out of the project during the last 6 months of my tenure at Jorhat, I was still monitoring and guiding the project group for its successful implementation.

I wish to write some conclusions about the Borolla-Khoraghat, 65km crude transfer pipeline. It was understood that the pipeline project suffered obstacles from locals in handing over ROU resulting in financial constraints to contractor due to cost overrun because of delay in execution. It was believed that vested interests were behind the obstacles and caused the project delay. However, with almighty God's blessings the pipeline was successfully commissioned after a period of 6 years from commencement and is now a prestigious asset of ONGC, Assam.

Other than the successful implementation of Khoraghat-Borolla 65km long trunk pipeline, the following major activities of onshore engineering services were handled and successfully done by me for the Jorhat asset/basin at ONGC.

8.3   Water Injection Facilities - Nambar

One of the assets at Nambar (Nambar GGS) was to be provided with water injection facilities, the conceptual plan was already completed and one major obstacle for tendering for the project facilities was the non-availability of soil investigation report for the facilities at Nambar GGS. The area ear- marked for the facilities was waterlogged, being used earlier for drill water storage. As the area was not getting dried up due to the frequent rains and getting filled up, soil investigation equipment could not be taken to site for investigation. Very soon after joining, I visited the site and understood the problem. Immediately, I visited the CSIR Lab at Jorhat and discussed with the soil investigation team and met the head of the Lab. I suggested to them to fabricate a float with empty drums by attaching them with straps at site and place the drilling equipment on the float over a moon-pool and conduct soil investigations as is done for offshore platform design. The CSIR Scientists agreed to the proposal and from ONGC we provided the float/ platform for the work. It was successfully done, and the data was later used for tendering and detailed engineering.

This work was pending for almost 2 years. My joining at Jorhat from offshore background helped in achieving the objective as soon as I joined.

Another work pending at Khoraghat GGS was metering facilities for the associated gas which was given to GAIL at the plant for marketing. Some approximate measuring was being done. I visited the plant several times and expedited the successful implementation of the metering facilities.

It was generally observed that as the posting of engineers from other regions to Assam was for three years, by the time a person joins and understand the requirement and plans the job, he gets transferred or the progress he made is slowed down after he leaves the station, which needs to be corrected. This may not be applicable for a 14 days on-off job pattern for drilling or plant operation.

Once when we were returning from the site, we had tea at Silonijaan, a place where we enter Nambar forest. It was getting dark as we entered the forest, when a herd of elephants was found to be suddenly moving towards our jeep from the front, one vehicle which was coming behind us cautioned us to take a U-turn and return. We were almost close to the elephants and somehow the driver could manage a U-turn very close to the elephants and drive back fast to Silonijaan. After some time, when a few more vehicles and some trucks gathered, we followed them and returned home. This was a thrilling experience during my tenure in Assam.

Another decision/methodology proposed by me during my tenure at Jorhat was very successful and later appreciated by all concerned. This was regarding road repairs done using the civil engineering services of ONGC at Khorghat, Nambar and

Kolaghat areas. Due to maximum vehicle movements by us, ONGC was regularly repairing the roads which were damaged, in these areas. Also, PWD, Assam was also undertaking their routine maintenance works as per their procedure. As the two agencies PWD and ONGC were engaged in this road repair work the actual condition of the roads was not satisfactory as they were done piece meal and they had excuses to blame each other. I suggested to the Basin manager, Jorhat that ONGC can estimate the annual expenditure incurred in such repairs and handover the amount to PWD, Assam and with this amount plus their budget the roads could be improved for longer life, and this was also agreed to by PWD. This was approved by the higher management of ONGC also. This was a good decision and led to better road conditions in that area of operation. Local people complaining about ONGC also stopped, as PWD could not pass on the criticism on ONGC for poor condition of roads.

* * *

Chapter 9

Back to Chennai, ONGC - Head Maint./ Engg. Services

I was transferred from Jorhat to Chennai in June 2008 and joined the technical Audit group which was almost non-existent at Chennai.

Within a short time of my joining at Chennai Shri.J.S.Sekhon, Basin Manager Cauvery, who was earlier Basin manager at Jorhat and who knew my work experience, created a Head Maintenance post at Chennai combining Civil and Electrical sections and I was made the Head Maintenance, an L-II post at Chennai for the first time. The job was as good as Head Engineering services, as construction projects for office and residential buildings were also part of the job. It was a great honour as my earlier works and contributions were recognized by Shri.J.S.Sekhon.

At Chennai, apart from regular maintenance of office buildings and Anna Nagar residential complex by electrical and civil engineers, the construction project consisting of an office complex, for RCC/RGL and residential buildings with 67 quarters and auditorium etc., for 2.5lakhs sq.ft was to be taken up for implementation within the Anna Nagar residential complex. As per the MOU with TNHB (Tamil Nadu Housing Board) the construction work was to be taken up by them as the land originally belonged to TNHB and was transferred to ONGC. Extensive interactions were held with TNHB officials for cost estimates, sanction of the project and tendering for the project through TNHB. They engaged CRN (CR Narayan Rao Associates) as architects for the project. I was involved in the project till tendering stage by TNHB. Best efforts were put in by interacting with RCC (Regional Computer Centre), RGL (Regional Geoscience Lab) and Infocom officers in finalizing the specifications, optimizing scope of work for their requirement and space allotments for the various sections in the office building. Similarly, for residential buildings, specifications and optimized layouts were drawn up in consultation with the HR department. The project was planned with a 3 * (three star) rating, green building concept. Effective project management strategies and meticulous scheduling & monitoring at various stages helped in achieving the completion of the project, though delayed to some extent beyond the planned schedule. It was a well-executed project considering the involvement of multiple stake holders, participants, clearances involved etc. This experience was useful when I was asked by NIOT to chair a committee for the development of Chithedu and Pimanji near Nellore for the Sea Front facility of NIOT, with a residential complex.

Apart from this major project, works such as replacement of air-conditioning system in 6th floor to 11th floor of CMDA building owned by ONGC, fixing of tiles on the old mosaic floor for the ONGC owned floors in Tower-1 and Tower-2 of CMDA buildings, procurement of new standby generator for ONGC at Tower-1 building, replacement of lifts in Tower-1 building were taken up during my tenure as Head Maintenance, between 2008-2012. Also, modern training halls were implemented in Tower-2 (8th floor) for the Regional Training Institute (RTI). The Basin Manager, Cauvery basin, Shri.J.S.Sekhon was very supportive to speed up the implementation of all these works for improvement of working conditions of ONGC executives as desired by him. He was one of the best task masters I had come across during my service. With the best support from him, OGCF (Oil and Gas conservation Fortnight) programs were conducted extensively during that time with talks by renowned experts and organizing awareness amongst the public in various modes.

In 2011, ONGC selected me for a management development program and trained me at IIM, Calcutta with an international tour of Europe to visit a few foreign companies, like TOTAL, France, OPEC, Vienna etc. It was a late selection, and I was amongst a junior batch. The training was for considering higher posts for the selected people. Unfortunately, that did not work out in my case, as from what I understood, probably my deputation to NIOT as Scientist-F, was a deterrent as projected by HR stalwarts. The same type of input from the HR department could be the reason why Mr. Subir Raha denied my extension for deputation, even with the request from Secretary, DOD in 2004.

9.1   Heading QAD - Southern Region

There was an unexpected transfer order to QAD section from engineering/maintenance in 2012. In fact, Head Maintenance was an L-II position and I/C-QAD, Chennai division is a L-III position. I guessed that it could be due to a small controversy with the Basin manager on a small contract on lift maintenance. As the ongoing maintenance contract was comingto an end and strict adherence to procedural matters was delaying the award of a fresh contract (the lift being an important item of usuage),

I had to extend the existing contract for 3 months on the same terms and conditions as approval from L1 did not come in time for this extension. What I followed was a pro-active approach as I learnt from a very senior stalwart which is also a mantra of Col. S.P.Wahi, former CMD, as you can see in his book "Leading from the front:" Quote: It is essential to have proper systems and procedures but one should not be a slave to them. When contingency demands in the interest of the organization, the leadership has to overlook the norms and act. Unquote. I didn't repent for it, as it was beneficial to the company. Personally, my local transfer was a blessing in disguise as I did not have to move to another location considering my health constraint.

WARNING MEMORANDUM

Shri P. Manivannan, DGM(M), CPF No.50144 while functioning as Head Maintenance was responsible for placement of Notification of Award of AMC with OTIS Elevators Co. Ltd. for 8 Nos. of OTIS lifts at Anna Nagar Residential colony w.e.f.01.10.2011 to 30.09.2014.

The committee constituted for enquiring on the procedural lapses and placement of notification of Award of AMC with OTIS Elevators Co. Ltd. pointed out the following procedural lapses while dealing the case file:

- " L1 approval not taken before placing LOA to OEM OTIS lifts.
- Case was not handled by MM Dept. and TC was not constituted for finalizing the contract as per procedure.
- Relevant instructions/amendments issued by ONGC are overlooked in constituting the TC

After going through the entire case on totality and keeping in view the facts and circumstances of the case, it is observed that there have been procedural lapses devoid of any malafide and no financial loss to ONGC.

In view of above lapses, **Shri P. Manivannan, DGM(M)** is hereby **warned** to be more careful while dealing such matters in future.

QAD is one of the best sections in ONGC because only suitably qualified and experienced people are posted and not just anyone with any kind of experience. This is different from ONGC's standard policy of distribution of discipline engineers in the name of job rotation for the areas of ONGC operations without consideration of experience or expertise in specific areas. ONGC never realized that such a policy is not correct to run a technical organization, the reasons for the same is only known to the experts of HR in ONGC and the management. International oil companies consider expertise for the relevant positions.

During 2012-2016, I was heading a group of talented engineers of Mechanical, Electrical and Electronics disciplines at locations in Chennai, Rajahmundry, Karaikal, and Hyderabad. Also, a new unit was started at Kakinada during my tenure but could not function as a full unit as the requirement of inspections were less and was managed by Rajahmundry unit itself. This was the status in 2015/16. However, now probably a separate QAD unit may be functioning at Kakinada, being a full fledged asset. The tenure in this section was smooth with new initiatives like drafting additional work instructions related to specific new items/ equipment which were earlier inspected with general instructions of a group of items. This was discussed in QAD review meetings and added, and this initiative was well received by all the centers of QAD and Chief Technical, Dehradun. I personally attended a few inspections and guided the inspectors for smooth and timely inspection.

During my tenure, QAD received the Golden Peacock award in 2014 from the Institute of Directors at Bangalore, mainly due to the achievement of my predecessors in the QAD, and I was also present as part of the award receiving team. Every Quarter, a  minimum of one visit was made to the centers at Rajahmundry, Karaikal and Hyderabad and reviewed the inspections made by the centers at random as per the laid down procedure of QAD.

It was a good experience inspecting two lathes for central workshop, Baroda at HMT, Cochin. The lathes were perfectly made to precision as per specifications and all measured parameters were within tolerance. Another mechanical engineer, Shri.J.M.Shankar, CE(M) and I were present and witnessed all the tests and measurements. HMT, Cochin had done a perfect job and I suggested repeat orders for other workshop units of ONGC.

9.2 Regional Training Institute

At the fag-end of my career with ONGC, when I was left with just 11 months of service, I was transferred to the Regional Training Institute. Here I was coordinating some training programs as a group head at Chennai Training Center as well as outstation programs for the various levels of employees of ONGC. An important work of development/framing of guidelines for skill development by ONGC under Pradhan Mantri Kaushal Vikas Yojana was undertaken (2016) along with the head of Regional Training Institute, Chennai Mr. Somesh Ranjan with inputs to Chennai unit and to headquarters for framing guidelines and capacity building. RTI was renamed as SDC (Skill Development Center). I retired from the services of ONGC on 31.03.2017 and continue with my social responsibility and knowledge sharing as much as I can practice.

* * *

Chapter 10

Social Responsibility and Knowledge Sharing

When I returned from Jorhat and joined ONGC, Chennai, in June 2008, after a few months of joining, Dr. M.A.Atmanand and Dr. G.A.Ramadass of NIOT, who were my junior colleagues when I was on deputation with NIOT came to my ONGC Chennai office and requested/suggested to me to apply for Director (NIOT) as the post was falling vacant. But knowing the constraints in ONGC for a second deputation and difficulties in resigning from ONGC, I suggested in turn that they can take up the post and wished them both. It so happened that both became Directors one after another and took NIOT forward. At that time, I assured them that I would extend my support and guidance to NIOT even while serving ONGC, and also thereafter.

As assured, I was able to join some of the NIOT's technical committees as member/chairman and extend my services, even today as of 2024, long after retirement.

The following are some such services rendered.

After the first desalination plant in Kavaratti Island was commissioned in 2005 (I was in NIOT 2001-2004) two more plants were established in Agatti and Minicoy by NIOT. During the establishment of Agatti and Minicoy plants considerable delays occurred due to reasons like redesign of structure in the wave breaking zone and logistic issues related to equipment etc. When UT Lakshadweep wanted 6 more LTTD plants to be installed on 6 more islands, a committee was formed by Director (NIOT) to suggest improvements for the future projects in those 6 islands. As chairman of the committee with members from IIT, NIO, CPWD and (UT Lakshadweep), member secretary Dr. M.V. Ramana Moorthy, inputs were given for the new project. I continue to be a member of the Technical Committee for this prestigious project of NIOT.

Further as Chairman of Project Review Board of Offshore Structures group, NIOT, headed by Dr. M.V. Ramana Murthy, I had the opportunity to review, advise and encourage the team of their works and services to the country. Other than the desalination plants of Lakshadweep islands, another important landmark project executed by the group, was the beach restoration project at the Pondicherry promenade. With members from Port Trust, CSIR, IIT(Civil and Ocean Engg.), it was a great experience for the review by members as well for the innovative design put up by Dr. Ramana Murthy's group. Though there were previous designs on the east coast with Groins, geotextile installation, break waters etc., which are conventional, and all methods have limitations and side effects and this new method was encouraged wholeheartedly by the committee. I personally had my confidence, considering the additional strength of data collection, study, design, and implementation, all done by the same agency i.e., NIOT. It was a successful project and details are available on YouTube. Some other notable works and consultancy services provided by this group to ports and other agencies were reviewed and suitable suggestions given by the board and personally it was very satisfying. Also when this group had a technical issue of surfacing of HDPE cold water pipeline in one of the LTTD plants, a safe and economical solution was given and successfully implemented and gave confidence to this group on their work.

Another important study undertaken by this group was on foundation designs for offshore wind turbines and economics of offshore wind energy for India. I had the opportunity to review and suggest some inputs on monopiles design and few other points towards economizing offshore wind energy projects in the Indian context, and feasibility studies were undertaken and reviewed.

Another group (Ocean Observation System group) headed by Dr. Venkatesan, a renowned scientist on weather monitoring and systems, desired my services as chairman of a standing committee on assessment of vandalism in moored buoys, in Indian waters and in the techno commercial evaluation of tenders for the services required for maintaining the data-buoys, in Indian waters.

I had the opportunity to get associated with a few other projects of NIOT like Autonomous Coring system for gas hydrates, DPR for 10 MLD floating LTTD plant, design of riser system for deep sea mining project (6000 m depth), manned submersible project etc. For the deep sea riser, a combination of drilling riser (as in a floater rig) and production riser (FPSO oil production system) a concept was

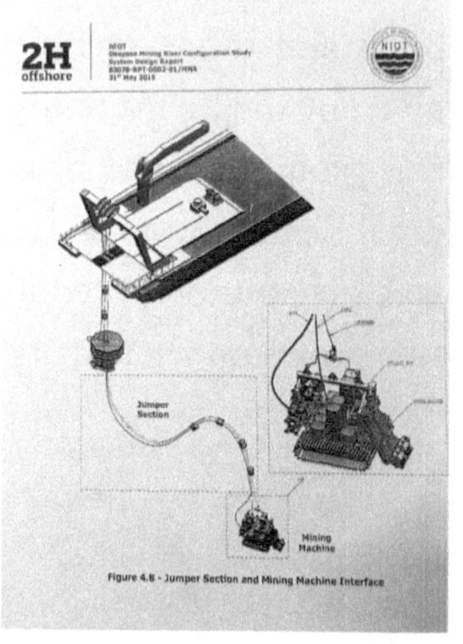

suggested and a design with analysis and methodology to lower and lift the riser assembly along with the mining machine was got done by a foreign design consultant, 2H Offshore who were experts in deep sea riser design. Though this design is specifically meant for demonstration only with the limitation of vessel availability with NIOT, however for commercial exploitation different version / model could be developed which are being discussed with scientists of NIOT by the author under the chairmanship of Dr. A.S. Kirankumar, former chairman, ISRO, a technical committee is evaluating the options to move forward on deep sea mining. As a member of this committee, I have been suggesting few techno commercially, viable alternatives as of 2024.

At the time of my retirement from ONGC (end of 2016), I was nominated as a member of Scientific Advisory Council of NIOT headed by Dr. P.S. Goel, former secretary, MOES, and continued the service for two terms.

Other than the above, I had the opportunity to motivate students at a few colleges in and around Chennai as a speaker, as Chief guest or as a guest lecturer(IIT, Ocean Engg. Dept, Kongu Engg. College, HIET, Institution Of Engineers etc). Lectures on offshore structures, renewable energy, project management, cost control, etc. were the general topics I covered as relevant to the audience. During my tenure at regional training institute, ONGC, I also motivated some students and shared some technical contents and experiences for their benefit. Shri G. Nallappan, GM(HR), now retired, was helping many students in their project work and coordinating with senior ONGC officers and sent them for motivation and training, relevant to their area of studies and I am thankful to him for participating in this noble work, joining hands with him. As part of ONGC's program on mentoring, I had also given mentoring lessons to a few junior colleagues during my tenure at Chennai, though it was my regular practice and attitude to mentor my subordinates and colleagues right from my joining ONGC and I used to mentor even contractor's and consultant's engineers who were associated with my project at various places.

Cost overrun (causes)

- Time overrun
- Imposition of unrealistic schedules
- Shortage of Talent in early project months
- Modified requirement / Specs change
- Escalation in costs matl./Labour/Eqpmt.
- Underfunding, either intentional or inadequate est.
- Inadequate market analysis
- Poor definition of requirements
- Under spec/over spec.
- Uncertainty about what you want.
- Challenging the state of art
- Sunk costs

Four steps to prevent cost overruns

- Establish the scope and features before beginning the work. A strong conceptual plan prior to start cost plan.

- Prepare your Technical Team to do its best

- Thoroughly investigate market capabilities and competition.

- Stay diligent to keep the project on right track

GS-15/23 offshore field development(case study)

Water depth	8-12 m
Monopiles	92" & 96"
Pipelines	4" & 6"
Proj.cost	11.7 MM$
Onshore Terminal	1 MM$
Str. Tonnage /Pltfm	300 MT
(normal pltfm 1000 -1200 MT)	
No of wells	2 each
Pile pen.	70 m
(Hydraulic hammer)	
completion	6 ½ months.
Design 1 month	
Fabn 4 months	
Tpt/instn 1 ½ months	
Features :	Tie-back exp. Wells
	Hatch in helideck
	1 well in pile
	Kevlar riser clamps
	Spiral stairs
	Self burial of p/l
Production	Gas 3 lakh m3/d
	Condensate 100 t/d

To conclude

- Things always take longer than you expect. No project can be repeated.
- A project is an adventurous inconvenience if rightly planned.
- And inconvenient adventure if inadequately planned
- Be right . Be adventurous.
- Best wishes.
- Thank u all

Apart from the above, I was a project guide to a few MBA students who were employees of ONGC/NIOT and taken up part time study from an open university which were mainly related to problem solving, with respect to oil and gas developments and renewable energy.

Another dimension of service was to assist the OBC association in ONGC as advisor, to mediate with management for developmental and supportive work to the public at large by receiving proportionate corporate social responsibility funds from ONGC and devise projects to promote education and economic development for deserving people. This was when I served at Chennai during 2011 to 2017.

I believe writing this book itself is a social responsibility to bring out what I had learnt from association with the stalwarts I came across during my career.

* * *

Chapter 11

An Analysis of the Title for This Book

With sincere thanks to the reader, I would like to submit a self-analysis of my career, life and the self-satisfaction achieved so that it may enable the readers to evolve their own path irrespective of hurdles and criticism without any compromise.

I came from scratch, which means that in an average normal course of life, I could have ended my life in a remote village without knowing much about what is the boundary of our country, what is patriotism, what is integrity, etc. It is God's grace and willingness that I studied well in school, which led to the teachers advising my father to send me for higher education beyond 11th standard.

At the next level, when I could only dream of becoming a school teacher to teach mathematics, as I was good at mathematics, senior friends took me to the next level, of studying engineering. At this level, it won't be an exaggeration to say that my father's advice and preaching which went deep into my mind had brought me to this level of a self-satisfied career and achievement. When I was to choose the branch of engineering it was very much my father's advice which influenced me to do mechanical engineering.

When I was to choose between a job or a PhD in the UK, it was again partly due to the need of the family and the desire to serve my country at the earliest was the key to my decision to take up the job. One piece of information I vaguely remember is that my father deposited about Rs. 230 (maybe, around the year 1970 I think) in the government of India Defence Bonds (Gold Bond) announced by the government for war needs though I was not aware of what it was at that time. Later it was returned as gold which was converted into a jewel for my sister. This had an impact on my young mind that everyone should contribute to the country when we grow up and earn.

Many times, during my early service in ONGC at Bombay and Chennai, though opportunities for working abroad came, my strong mind didn't allow such diversions as I felt that it was not right for me to choose that option, and I would fail in my duty to the country and to the advice of my father if I chose that. Though many friends who left for green pastures abroad are now financially and status-wise well above me, I feel proud where I am.

Even when the joint venture oil companies came into India, when the first opportunity came to me before many other colleagues who left, it was the same driving force which made me to continue with ONGC. At that time, my discussions with my wife and her support of my wish and aim in my career needs to be mentioned as part of this book. I annexe a story which was written by her during this time and sent to Anantha Vikatan, a

Tamil weekly for publishing (but not published) for appreciation of her support.

She sacrificed her career and learnt to live without the normal ambitions of an average woman. At the time of my marriage, my wife was employed in the Social Welfare Department in the government of Pondicherry. Even when I was transferred to the south, the initial idea was to take my transfer to Karaikal so that she could continue her service there as it comes under Pondicherry. But my interest to continue in offshore construction projects by joining at Chennai, could not support her continuance in her service. She couldn't continue her job, in social welfare, though later she served as part time lecturer by teaching nutrition to Nursing students of the prestigious Apollo group of institutions. When financial constraints were experienced because I had to support my extended family, we also made revisions in the budget with more restrictions and did not choose the path of higher earnings by joining private JV companies.

Though my siblings and their families could not be fully satisfied meeting their financial requirements, this was the balance we could make, within the boundaries of my chosen principles and my earnings. This condition prevailed until the 2007 pay revision was implemented by ONGC. If I had chosen to work abroad or by joining any private joint venture companies, probably, I could have added more wealth to my family and extended much more support to my extended family. But the deterring force of my principles always succeeded.

It is my strong opinion that national wealth and minerals should not be shared with foreign entities, only their services could be hired at a cost. The policy of privatization of oil fields has not yielded any positive outcome as can be seen. This aspect had been dealt with very clearly in the book "Leading from the Front". To avoid controversy, I do not want to write more on this topic.

I leave it to the readers the justification or otherwise of the title, by going through my journey. My only wish to the readers is to preach patriotism to young minds. If this effort to bring out this book ignites at least a few minds to cherish the happiness and satisfaction of being patriotic, i.e., give more and take less policy, it would be a great success.

I hope engineers, scientists, and other readers may also gain some beneficial insight in the technical aspects and practices shared here with my experiences. I have mentioned many stalwarts who had contributed much more with whom I had associated during my journey and what I had done may be a small fraction compared to their contribution. But this small book is also meant to commend their support, service and contribution. Only two from the many names I had mentioned in this book, I would like to bring out for the reader's reference.

One is a small brief about late Shri. K. Anjaneyan, who retired as Regional Director, from erstwhile Southern Regional Business Centre of ONGC (SRBC). He groomed many engineers and preached honesty and patriotism, and he was a great model to be emulated. His one great advice to follow is when systems and procedures fail to protect the company's interest, we can overlook such procedures and do the right thing and take timely and right decisions to protect the company's interest. This is more or less the same view of Dr. Col.S.P.Wahi, former CMD, ONGC as I could gather from his book. Though I am not able to produce the exact language of his communication, I followed his advice and was proud to be his follower. I have referred to him at some places in the book. I had the opportunity to interact with him both in Bombay and Chennai, and even after his retirement, whenever he visited the ONGC office and on the phone.

A brief of the lecture notes jointly prepared by me and reviewed by him is placed as an annexure.

Another person I would like to mention is the founder director of NIOT, Prof. M. Ravindran. Though I had only a few years of close association with him I admired every quality of his as a teacher, scientist and leader taking along all the members of the team from top to bottom. My association and interaction with him woke up the scientist instinct in me and made me to realize that I should have chosen a full-fledged career as a scientist. His strong desire to prove Ocean Thermal Energy Conversion Technology as a potential renewable energy sources on a larger scale, his tireless spade work and devoted efforts have paved the way for the people of Lakshadweep islands to get good drinking water through LTTD technology, which is a spin-off technology from OTEC.

In a book "Renewable Energy Sources, their impact on Global Warming and Pollution" by renowned authors, they have referred to my name also, along with Prof. Ravindran, as proponents of OTEC. I felt apprehensive as my contribution to OTEC is negligible except co-authoring few papers and leading the OTEC team for a while for deployment and demonstration of his dream project, the world's first1MW pilot plant in India.

Everyone named here in this book has given me valuable input towards my successful career, apart from their contributions to society.

Some names are not mentioned either due to loss of memory or the relevant content of the associated services with them is not written in the book.

Some comments brought out in this book about the company or anyone's opinion or decision etc., are not meant to criticize, but only with the intention that they can be lessons for future correction and benefits.

* * *

About Myself

1. Educational Outline
1st Standard to 5th Standard (1962 - 1967)

My first school was a remote one with 2 teachers for 5 classes at Vinayagapuram village, Semangalam Mathura, Vanur PO & TK now in Villupuram District, earlier under undivided South Arcot district.

- Regular to school.

- Even on the day of my uncle's marriage in our house, I attended school. Everyone was searching in the function only to find me in the school.

- Born on 12-5-1957, the date of birth was changed to 12-3-1957, as I had to complete 5 years to be admitted to the 1st standard in school.

6th Standard to 8th Standard (1967 - 1970)

- Semangalam village, where only classes up to 8th standard was available.

- Daily walk up/down 3km each direction to and from school.
- 1st rank in class, from 6th onwards known; my rank during the earlier years was not known, though teachers used to say good and appreciated me often.
- The class teacher advised me to take part in oration, recitation, acting etc., preferred only recitation.
- Showed poor interest in sports, often got tired soon in sports activities.
- Escaped drowning in a well while washing utensils after lunch. Due to timely help by a senior student, I survived.

9th Standard to 11th Standard (1970 - 1973)

- Gandhi High School, Tiruchitrambalam Koot Road, about 7km from home.
- Initially travelled by bus for a few months as I did not have a bicycle.
- Later, a cycle (Raleigh) was purchased by my father from an EB lineman. The cycle was ridden by another student with me on the pillion.
- Learnt to ride the cycle only in the village after nearly 1 year of purchase.
- Always stood 1st in class.
- As earlier mentioned, exhibited poor interest in sports.
- Won prizes in literary competitions, recitation, Tamil poem writing etc.

(1973 - 1974) PUC

- Government Arts College, Cuddalore.

- First time went out of home staying alone (with new boys of same age group) in Devanampattinam, a village near the beach and close to the college.

- Shri. Ramasamy and Shri. Perumal became my close associates and guides, being my seniors in B.Sc & B.Com 1st year. Shri Ramasamy's father worked in Neyveli Lignite Corporation and hence the idea of becoming an engineer was inculcated by him for my better future. His family became close to our entire family and he continued to guide me. His association was a major milestone and turning point in my education.

- Stood 1st in PUC, Maths, Physics, Chemistry group.

- Initially found it difficult to catchup with the English medium instruction as I had studied in Tamil medium till 11th standard.

- However, I picked up within 2 to 3 months & started scoring top marks in Maths, Physics and Chemistry.

- Got the 1st prize in annual day of the College for Academic excellence.

(1974 - 1979) B.E

- Government College of Engineering, Salem

- Though I never had an idea, hope or aim to do engineering as neither of my parents nor any close relatives were aware of such a possibility or ability to get admission.

- Shri. Ramasamy guided me to apply for B.E.

- I attended an interview at the College of Engineering, Guindy Campus. Shri. Ramasamy accompanied me.

- Stayed at a Casuarina Wood Store (Firewood) in Pallavaram the previous night owned by a person known to my father and an old business associate Shri. K.E. Sambandam Chettiar. I travelled to Guindy by train from Pallavaram.

- I had breakfast at the Guindy Railway Station. I ate 2 to 3 bananas to boost my weight to avoid getting rejected in physical fitness tests.

- The interview was very successful. Former Vice Chancellor, Dr. V. Kulandaisamy took the interview with 2 others(define, phi examples for element & compound and a few other general questions about family, education etc.). I answered all correctly with presence of mind, specifically for the first one, I didn't have a definition in fluent English, though it was correct. Appreciated by Chairman, he had no further questions, only a smile to other members if they had any other questions.

- While waiting for the result of the interview for B.E admission(though I was confident) many advised me to seek admission for B.Sc. Maths or Physics as B.E admission was difficult.

- Brother Ramasamy's confidence boosted our confidence further, including my father's.

- I also attended an interview for B.E in Annamalai University but finally was not selected there for B.E. Chemical Engg.

- Travelled up & down to Neyveli Township (Ramasamy's home) a few times during the stressful days till admission results were published.

- It was a great day to see my roll no. in B.E admission list in Malaimurasu Paper.

- The entire family, close associates and relatives were very happy to know that I was selected and to be the 1st engineer in the area surrounding the villages.

- After receiving the admission card, I travelled to Salem Engineering College accompanied by my father and Shri. Ramasamy.

- One great surprise during the joining was that the Cuddalore Arts College English Professor's (Shri. Periasamy) son M.P.Bala Subramanian (who studied PUC at St. Josephs College, Trichy) also joined at the same time with me at GCE, Salem for the B.E degree course. Shri.M.P.Bala Subramanian joined BHEL Trichy after M.Tech at IIT, Madras.

- Shri. Ramasamy introduced a senior at College, Mr. Rajan, who took care of me initially to escape ragging.

- The 5-year course period for B.E at GCE, Salem was memorable though financial setbacks (this is common in any average agricultural family as there is no steady income and cash flow) led to defaulting of mess bill and had to go out to eat in canteen & Mani's tiffin shop at the entrance of the college.

- My leisure activities during college were writing short stories and poems, even winning prizes and publishing in college magazines.

- The third year branch selection was crucial, preferred mechanical engineering to lead a career in Power Production as in Neyveli Lignite Corporation, or the state Electricity Department in a power plant. My father's interest was that I should study electrical engineering and give free power connection without taking any bribe to agricultural pump sets to farmers. This was the limited exposure and motive we had at the time of choosing the branch, though I was eligible for any branch, even Electronics and Telecommunication, for which we had to shift to some other college. As mechanical Engg. meets the criteria of my father and my interest, I opted for that.

- In the third year B.E Mechanical class, I got 75.75%, so applied for B.E(Hons).

- I could not complete B.E(Hons) due to lower percentage of marks in 4th and final year due to reasons such as:

- Defaulting of mess fees and needed to eat outside, often 2 times a day (friends like Mr. Krishnaraj took me for lunch as guest). As mentioned earlier an agriculturists earnings is not regular income and hence timely availability of money is a constraint for them, this is still worse for agriculturists today and hence many of them sell their lands to educate their children which is a pity.

- I missed classes sometimes.

- Health deterioration also added to lower marks.

- In one of the exams, I scored just 50% and passed as my health was bad and wrote the exam with a half-conscious mind.

- Shri.Ramasamy came to GCE, Salem and stayed with me to support me during exams in view of my bad health.

- Designing a Grain Thresher was the project work. It was jointly done with friends M/s Malaichamy, Ramasamy, Robin Packiaraj. Malaichamy joined NLC (& then joined a company in Gujarat). Later he converted to Christianity & became a Paster. Ramasamy (called as Professor) joined Metrowater, Chennai & retired. Robin Packiaraj worked in a private company, Chennai, and then moved to Dubai.

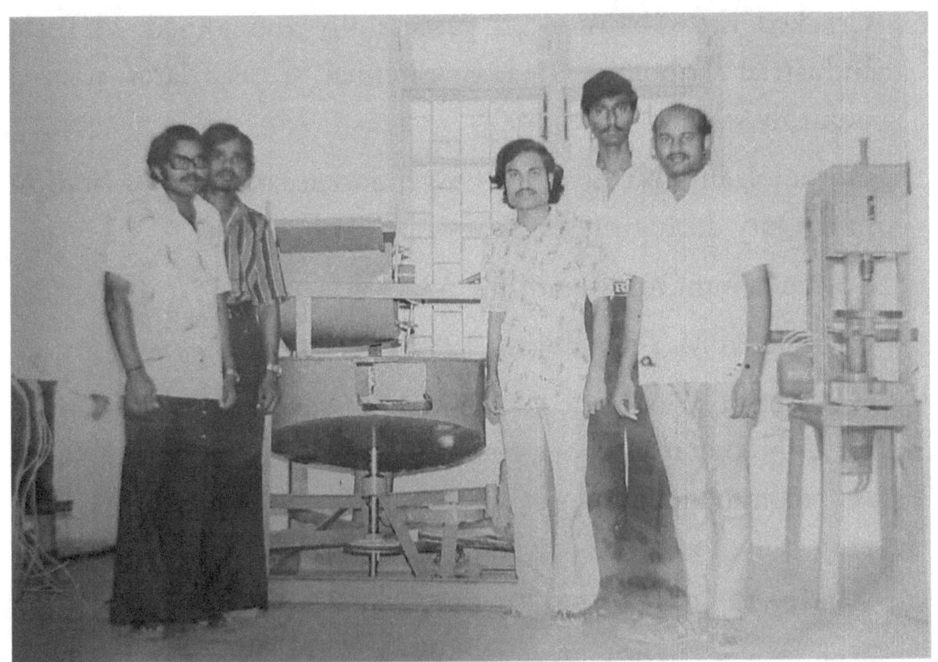

- SBI offered a loan of Rs. 10 lakhs to implement the project as an entrepreneur. However, I dropped the idea as no one was keen on this and raising even margin money for the venture was not easy with our background.

- After completion of the course, a job was not available immediately except for some students.

- Got an appointment in SAIL, Bhilai, but did not join. I could not get a job of our choice at a nearby place as desired by parents.

- I joined as an apprentice for Rs. 290/- stipend, at PWD Chepauk; used to visit some sites in North Madras.

- Till that time, I was not well aware of M.Tech courses at IIT; it was also not thought of during the B.E course study. After seeing some friends of GCE, Salem, I thought of joining IIT, Chennai, and wrote the CEPA entrance exam.

- Cracked the CEPA exam successfully and joined M.Tech. Industrial Tribology at IIT, Chennai, a year later with a monthly stipend of Rs. 600.

- Got a job in TNEB, as in charge, Sarkarpathy Power Station near Ooty during my 1st year of M.Tech. course.

- I did not want to discontinue M.Tech.

- Completed M.Tech. during 1980-82.

- Got jobs in Bi-Metal Bearings Coimbatore, Lubrizol, Bombay for Tribology related placements. Also got selected in ONGC. As recommended by prof. B.S. Prabhu, my Guide for M.Tech project, I chose ONGC.

- Went to ONGC, Dehradun in March '82 for joining and came back for completion of project work at IIT, Madras.

- The ONGC Manager at KDMIPE, advised me to join after completing the course and gave extension to join on 1/7/82.

- This put me in a place below all those who joined in March-May'82, which might have affected the career with delayed promotion & loss of a promotion even at the end of career as this is one of the causes in addition to ONGC's, ever changing Promotion Policies.

- Also got opportunity for admission in Imperial College of Science & Technology, London as recommended and suggested by a visiting professor Prof. Cameron, who used to give special lectures during M.Tech. course, for doing Phd in Elasto-hydrodynamics based on my M.Tech. project results "Grease lubrication of Journal bearing" with Grease as a flowing lubricant. I could not choose that due to my family situation and circumstances. Besides, working abroad was not in my plan even if I went for higher studies abroad.

- Finally joined ONGC on 1/7/82 at Dehradun as AEE(Mech) leaving all other options.

Various positions held in ONGC / NIOT

Year	Position	Remarks
1982 -1986	AEE (Mech) E1	ONGC, Mumbai
1987 -1990	EE (Mech) E2	ONGC, Mumbai
1992 - 1995	DYSE (Mech) E3	ONGC, Chennai
1996 - 2000	SE (Mech) E4	ONGC, Chennai
2001 - 2005	CE (Mech) E5	ONGC, Chennai
	Scientist F (E*)	NIOT, Chennai
2006 - 2017**	DGM (Mech) E6	ONGC, Johrat,
ONGC, Chennai (Redesignated as GM)		

*** Norms for elevation from E6 to E7 is four years, E7 to E8 three years, E8 to E9 two years. This explains Mr. MRN.Swamy's comment, slow (no?) growth in the parent organization (unknown reasons).*

Advisory Positions

Year	Position	Remarks
2010	Chairman, Technical Committee for improvements on LTTD Plants at Lakshadweep	NIOT
2011-2013	Member - Technical Review committee DPR of 10 MLD Offshore Desalination Plant	NIOT
2012 - 2018	Chariman, Project Review Board, Ocean Structure Group	NIOT
2012 - 2017	Chairman, Assessment of Vandalism committee - moored data buoys	NIOT,
2012 - 2018	Member, Joint Monitoring Group - Autonomous Coring System for Gas Hydrate	NIOT

Year	Position	Remarks
2015 - 2017	Chairman, Project Review & Co-ordination Committee, Sea -front facility, Nellore	NIOT
2015	Chairman, DPR for offshore numerical tank	NIOT
2015	Chairman, Deep sea mining riser configuration study	NIOT
2016 - 2022	Member, Scientific Advisory Council	NIOT
2018 - ****	Member, TCEC, 6 LTTD Plants - Lakshadweep	NIOT

2. Family Tree

Why this chart: To depict the result of determination of minimally educated parents (Mother could not read or write, father informal education, Thinnaipallikudam) of a remote village how it transformed the further generations and to encourage writing by similar growth stories for the benefits of the society.

Father: S.N. PARASURAMA GOUNDAR (Agriculturist)

Mother: P. VIJAYALAKSHMI

Village: Vinayagapuram, Vanur P.O and TK, Villupuram District, Tamil Nadu.

(Father knows to read and write in Tamil, he was good at old Tamil epics, Ramayan, Mahabharath and songs of Thirupugazh, Pattinathar etc. (all old literature). Though I have not seen any of his performance on stage, he was a Therukoothu artist who preached ethics to village people, as I understood, in his performances with the poems and verses. That was his educational background. I had seen other Therukoothu teams performing in my village wherein some performers used to praise him and take his blessings before they performed. Also he was known for his dispute resolution strategy in joint families smoothly during partition and other family matters and was invited for such meetings at nearby villages, as Nattamai. I had witnessed few such proceedings wherein he convinced all stake holders with his judgements and with a happy ending.

Siblings

1) P. MANIVANNAN (self)
2) P. KAMALAKANNAN (Brother)
3) P. PANJAVARNAM (Sister)
4) P. KARUNAKARAN (Brother)

P. MANIVANNAN Family

1) P. MANIVANNAN, M.Tech
2) SHEELA MANIVANNAN, M.Sc., M.Phil., M.Ed.,
3) KALYAN SUNDER MANIVANNAN, B.E., MS(USA)
4) SHYAM SUNDER MANIVANNAN, B.E., MS(USA)

P. KAMALAKANNAN Family

1) P. KAMALAKANNAN, PUC(Pre-University)
2) K. VALARMATHI (alias) CHANDRA
3) K. PARIMELALAGAN, BA, LLB
4) K. PARTHASARATHY, B.B.M, M.BA
5) Dr. Major K. PRABAKARAN, M.B.B.S., M.D.,

P. PANJAVARNAMFamily

1) G. GNANASEKARAN, B.A.,
2) G. PANJAVARNAM

3) G. VIJAYAKUMAR, B.Sc., M.B.A.,
4) G. SOWMYA, M.Sc., M.Phil., B.Ed.,
5) G. ELAYARAJA, B.E., M.Tech.,

P. KARUNAKARAN Family

1) P. KARUNAKARAN, B.Sc., M.A., B.Ed.,
2) K. GOUNDHI, M.Sc., M.Phil., B.Ed.,
3) K. DHARSHINI, B.D.S.,
4) K. MEGAVARSHINI, B.Tech.,

(Family tree expanding with more additions and further new members/additions not included here)

* * *

Appendices / Annexures

Management of Offshore Contracts
Special Features Viz-a-Viz Contract Provisions
Shri. K. Anjaneyan / P.Manivannan

Introduction

In the late 70's ONGC commenced development of Bombay High Offshore Field which was the first Offshore Development Project which even today is the largest offshore field in India. More than 120 well platforms and 15 process complexes along with associated pipelines and Oil Loading Systems, SPM's and trunk pipelines to land terminal etc., have been installed. The execution of offshore projects through international contractors by international competitive bidding is of specialised nature and the salient features of the same are discussed here.

Type of Bidding

After the approval of the scheme, offshore works are split into projects of convenient sizes for handling and tender documents are prepared along with technical specification for issue to international competitive bidders. Bids are normally invited in two bid system i.e. Technical Bid and Commercial Bid sealed separately. A technical short list is made before opening of the price bid and finally the successful bidder is selected for award of work for execution of the project. Invariably a pre-bid conference is held among the prospective bidders to explain the bid requirement for better understanding of the project by the bidders. Also, clarificatory discussions are held with the bidders after opening the technical bids to clarify the points raised by the bidders and to obtain details and capabilities of the bidders towards final short-listing of the bidders technically.

Clarity of specifications and contract conditions are very important to achieve the successful completion of the project without cost and time overruns and also for smooth co-ordination with the contractor. Offshore Contract being of a specialised nature many special conditions are included as provisions in the contract. A bid evaluation criteria covering technical and commercial conditions to be fulfilled by the contractor is published in the bid package.

Bid Evaluation Criteria

Bid Evaluation Criteria is classified under two heads namely, Technical and Commercial. As part of Technical Bid Evaluation Criteria a minimum experience of the bidder in the execution of offshore projects of similar complexities and magnitude will be considered as the top most criteria for selection of the bidder. Also, a sub-contractor proposed by him for a particular part should also have a relevant experience. Other technical criteria shall cover items such as bidders proposed barges, marine equipment acceptance to certain minimum requirement, mobilisation of constructional plant and equipment as per technical requirement and to meet any contingency at offshore etc.

Various commercial conditions are also stipulated for short-listing the bidders, insisting that the bidders are advised not to take deviations on important clauses such as completion, performance guarantee, contract price, duties and taxes, insurance and liability, payment procedure and force majeure etc.

Certain criteria for loading of bids is also published to apply proper loading of price bids in case bidders take certain deviations on clauses such as weather down time, structural tonnage variation, pipeline length variation etc.,

Special Features

1. Knowledge of Site Conditions

The foremost and general obligation of the contractor towards knowledge of site conditions needs to be clearly spelt in the contract. Though the contractor may be submitting his bids based on the information fumished in the bid package with respect to Hydrological, Sub-surface, Climatic and Physical conditions of the site, it is essential that contractor should be advised to satisfy himself with the information furnished in the bid package and if necessary to make inspection of site and surroundings and collect additional information to satisfy himself the form and nature thereof regarding the sub-surface, Hydrological and climatic condition, the quantities and the nature of the work and materials necessary for the completion of the works.

The company normally furnishes in the bid package, the weather data during installation conditions and operating/extreme storm condition at site. Soil data at platform location and pipeline route is also furnished. Nevertheless the contractor is advised to carry out a pre-engineering survey before detailed engineering work as part of contractors scope of work.

It is the responsibility of the company to specify the offshore working season, limiting installation conditions, site specific environmental data etc to advise the contractor for choosing the right marine spread and plan their activities and schedule, including right choice of work centres for various activities.

2. Constructional Plant and Equipment

As the quality of the marine spread and constructional plant and equipment mobilised by the contractor at site is very important, the contract clause should provide for stringent conditions to refrain the contractor from mobilising the plant and equipment susceptible to break-downs. Contract Clause should cover that if the contructional plant and equipment is inadequate or found to be not suitable, he should mobilise another suitable marine spread/ equipment to complete the works in time. Also it is necessary to indicate that the contractor shall bear the weather downtime during the defined working season for the area/site, which otherwise leads to contractual complications and extra claims

3. Survey Requirement

Though the company provides certain basic survey data for bid work, for carrying out detailed engineering the contractor shall be advised to undertake independently pre-engineering survey of the site conditions, such as water depth, seabed topography, existing platforms and pipelines, wellheads etc before detailed engineering work. The contractor shall be advised to carry out pre-construction/pre- installation survey prior to installation work and post construction survey after installation works.

4. FACILITIES ON CONSTRUCTION SPREAD.

It is mandatory to incorporate clauses to advise the contractor to mobilise equipments like pile jetting, pile top drilling equipment, grouting equipment and support diving equipment including video monitoring etc. Helicopter landing facilities on the barge and transportation and accommodation facilities for company representative during supervision of works also needs to be specified in the contract.

5. COMPLIANCE TO LAWS

Contractor shall be clearly advised to acquaint himself with all the laws of the land and procedures and formalities of the Indian Government Agencies such as customs and excise, licencing authorities, DGH, Navy and Coast Guard etc., Specific clauses with respect to the above should be clearly included in the contract. The contractor shall be advised on offshore pollution responsibility, refraining him from generating any pollution at work site and to comply with the pollution responsibilities. The contractor shall also be advised to insure against claims on pollution or contamination.

6. MEASUREMENT OF WORK

All offshore works are measured based on as installed basis. Platform structural tonnage adjustment is measured based on installed weight basis and pipeline length are measured based on as laid basis and payment is adjusted accordingly.

7. GUARANTEE CONDITIONS

To ascertain the quality of materials, equipments and components used in the execution of works, guarantee conditions are specified for the entire works and for supporting structures including design guarantee for the facilities till the design life. Normally a 12 month warranty period from the date of issue of certificate of completion is specified.

8. CONSULTANT/CERTIFICATION AGENCIES

Contract clause shall specify the role of Consultants and Certification Agencies and the Contractor's responsibilities in meeting the requirements of the Consultant / Certification Agencies in the Project at various stages of the Project indicating the responsibility of the Contractor to co-ordinate with the Consultant/ Certification Agency for implementation of the Project as per Bid specifications. This clause shall also cover the duration of approval cycle for various works and access for inspection, etc. for timely completion and quality control as per bid requirements.

9. COMPLETION-DELAY/LIQUIDATED DAMAGES

This clause shall be framed in such a way that the Contractor is motivated to complete the Project in time or ahead of schedule. It would be encouraging if the Contractor is given a Bonus for early completion and a pre-determined levy of Liquidated damages is applied for delay in completion. However in ONGC only levy of LD upto 10% maximum is applied for delay in works.

10. CHANGE ORDERS/ VARIATIONS

For variations with respect to increase/decrease in tonnage of structures and increase/decrease in length of pipelines adjustment rates should be available as per the price bid. However, for change orders which cannot be pre-determined in terms of time and cost has to be mutually discussed and agreed with the company and the contractor. For this purpose, suitable clauses for clear execution of change order are required to be incorporated including the procedure for such change orders.

In the execution of turn key contracts, certain change orders may be raised by the contractors due to improper understanding of the company's requirements at the bidding stage or due to wrong interpretation of specifications due to ambiguity. To avoid such situations it is necessary to furnish the detailed specifications and drawings as clear as possible and it is all the more important to indicate an order of priority for reference in case of any discrepancy between drawings and specifications etc. The following order of priority is generally preferred for clarity.

Design Criteria
Equipment Specifications
Drawings
General Specifications
Codes and Standards

11. PAYMENT PROCEDURE/MILESTONE FORMULA

In turn key contracts it is essential to provide suitable clauses hi-lighting the payment procedures to be followed including the billing schedule/milestone formula. In the offshore projects a milestone formula based on the price bid submitted by the contractor is evolved and included in the contract which will be followed for payment.

12. PROJECT INSTRUCTIONS

It is essential to include the project instructions outlining the duties and responsibilities of the project participants and the procedures, rules and regulations and other requirements of the Company relating to the performance of the work and services by the contractor. Under the project instructions it is necessary to indicate the appointment of consultant by the company and their role during the project execution, approvals required to be taken by the contractor, submission of documents to various agencies and specified time interval for review and approval of design, AFC drawings, purchase specification, data sheet as per bid document, procurement of spare parts, operating manuals etc, Other details such as correspondence procedure, address for communication, delivery of materials to designated addressee, distribution of correspondence, submission of progress report, safety report etc, shall also be detailed.

13. CONTRACT MANAGEMENT DURING PROJECT EXECUTION

Even if a proper contract is formulated and signed between the parties unless it is properly monitored during the project execution by an experienced team of executives the project success cannot be guaranteed. The project team should be thorough in the contract conditions, technical requirements, specifications and drawings, codes and standards relevant to the works etc. If the company's team is inadequate in certain areas, it is preferable to appoint a consultant to seek advise on the specialised areas of work.

Upon award of LOI to the selected party a kick off meeting should be called, to discuss and firm up the detailed schedule, works centres for various activities, organogram of the contractor, equipments and marine spread proposed etc. The contractor should be advised to sign the contract as soon as possible not later than a months time. Also the milestone formula for payment should be finalised and incorporated in the contract before signing.

During the detailed engineering phase, the contractor shall be advised to raise in the form of technical queries for any clarifications on design criteria, specifications, drawings etc and finalisation of vendors for supply of equipments, materials etc., Company representatives and consultant representatives are deputed to the engineering centre for review of detailed engineering. To maintain the schedule priority of engineering works for the ordering of long lead items, bulk materials, structural steel etc, are to be taken up. Project team shall constantly review the engineering progress to match with the overall schedule and take corrective action as and when required

Similar to the Engineering works, project team shall depute company representatives and consultant representatives to the fabrication site for supervision during fabrication. It is the responsibility of the company's representatives to ascertain that the facilities incorporated /erected are as per the specifications which suits the requirements of various departments such as operations group, reservoir group, drilling group etc., Proper dimensional control and quality control in welding and materials are essential during fabrication. Load out, transportation and installation engineering works are to be critically examined before the activities and contingency procedures need to be developed for any eventuality. A HAZID report identifying the hazards in installation, causes and safeguards need to be analysed and responsibility to be specified for implementing the recommendations of the HAZID report for safe load out, transportation and installation of the facilities. During installation and pre- commissioning, company representatives experienced in various disciplines are to be deputed for supervising the works.

CONTRACT SETTLEMENT

On completion of the project it is necessary to settle the contract as quickly as possible within a fixed time frame to avoid interest payment, contractual complication etc., It is necessary to have a post contract settlement meeting with the contractor to come to a conclusive settlement. Settlement of issues related to liquidated damages for delay in works, if any adjustment for tonnage variations, pipeline length variations, change orders and cost benefit items needs to be discussed with the contractor and finalised expeditiously so that the contract can be closed amicably.

P. MANIVANNAN
ONGC.Chennai.
(Formerly Scientist - F & Mission-Head. For OTEC,
National Institute Of Ocean Technology,
Ministry of Earth Sciences, India).
Correspondence: pmanivannanongc@rediffmail.com).

OCEAN THERMAL ENERGY CONVERSION (OTEC) A PROMISING SOURCE FOR ENERGY SECURITY OF INDIA

Introduction

Renewable energy was the only source of energy available for mankind untill the past few hundred years prior to the discovery of fossil fuels. Though unfortunately we call the renewable energy used by man since thousands of years as non-conventional energy and call the non-renewable fossil fuels as conventional energy, which is a misnomer, our endeavor should be to return back to the happy era of renewable energy and call them rightly as conventional energy.

The transition from renewable to fossils, to fuel the present economies, has eroded the environment, leading to global warming, green house gases, polluting the atmosphere, etc. and the survival of the fittest is in danger now, leave alone the other forms of life. It is the moral responsibility of the present society to correct the mistakes and to handover at-least the partly disturbed present to the future generations without further deterioration. This necessity forced a number of countries to reorient and to rediscover the renewable energy sources which is mainly derived from the sun, the ultimate source of energy.

Ocean Thermal Energy is a promising source of renewable energy which can be built in larger capacities than any other renewable source of energy. Even though OTEC research started as early as 1970, advancement and commercialization of OTEC has not taken place due to less interest shown by developed countries as fossil fuels are available at competitive prices and OTEC research advanced only whenever oil price soared. Another reason for the slow progress of OTEC technology is that the best potential for OTEC resources are available to small island communities and developing countries whose funding capacity for research is limited. Though Ocean Thermal Energy is not known to many of us, compared to Wind or Solar Energy, this source of energy is also derived from solar energy in an indirect form.

Ocean Thermal Energy-principle

The sun warms the oceans at the surface and the wave motion mixes the warmed water downward to depths of about 100 m. This mixed layer is separated from the deep cold water, formed at high latitudes, of 1000 m. by a thermo cline. The resulting vertical temperature distribution therefore consists of two layers separated by an interface with temperature differences between them ranging from 100C to 250 C. The higher values are found in equatorial waters. Ocean Thermal Energy Conversion is an energy technology that converts solar radiation to electric power using the temperature difference between the warm surface water and the cold deep sea water by operating a heat engine (Fig.1). It is estimated that the amount of solar power absorbed by Oceans is equivalent to at least 4000 times the amount of energy presently consumed by humans. For a conversion efficiency of 3% from Ocean Thermal energy to electricity, we would need only 1% of this renewable energy to meet the total demand of our present requirement.

There are basically three types of OTEC processes: closed cycle, open cycle and hybrid cycle based on the thermo dynamic process. There are many efforts in the past for optimizing the cost of OTEC using power cycle analysis.

Ocean Thermal Energy Conversion by a closed cycle, where a low boiling point liquid like Ammonia/R-32/R-134a is used as the working fluid for thermo dynamic conversion of heat into power, is the preferred option against a open cycle. The heat transferred from the warm surface water causes the working fluid to evaporate. The expanding vapour drives a turbine attached to a generator which produces electricity. Cold sea water passing through a condenser containing the vapourised working fluid turns the vapour back into liquid, which is then recycled through the system (Ref. diagram). The by-products of Ocean thermal energy conversion are desalinated water, air-conditioning and aqua-culture. (Cold sea water is rich in nutrients). Open cycle OTEC plant uses the warm surface water itself as the working fluid. The water vaporizes in a near vacuum at surface water temperatures. The expanding vapour drives a low-pressure turbine attached to a generator, which produces electricity. The vapour, which has lost its salt and is almost pure fresh water, is condensed back into a liquid by exposure to cold temperatures from deep ocean water. If the condenser keeps the vapour from direct contact with sea water, the condensed water can be used for drinking water, irrigation or aquaculture.

Ocean Thermal Energy -status

Luis A. Vega who has done extensive research and analysis on OTEC recommends as follows:

"Given that it takes decades for new energy technologies to reach maturity, it seems sensible to consider ocean thermal resource as a renewable fuel for the future. At first OTEC plant-ships providing electricity via submarine power cables, to shore stations would be implemented. This would be followed in 20-30 years, with OTEC factories deployed along equatorial waters producing energy intensive products, like ammonia and hydrogen as the fuels that would support the post fossil-fuel era."

Lockeed Martin, a US based company is progressing on an OTEC pilot plant with funding from US navy. Few small island nations are also working on establishing commercial OTEC plants. In August 2015 the world's largest operating OTEC plant (100 KW) has been grid connected to a US electrical grid in Hawaai. In April 2013 an agreement was signed for a10MW OTEC plant installation on the southern coast of China between Beijing based Reignwood Group and Lockheed Martin. A 10 MW floating OTEC plant is in progressed state and expected to operate in Martinique/Bellefontaine by DCNS France consortium. The Indian Navy plans to go green by setting up a 20MW OTEC plant to power its base in the ecologically sensitive Andaman & Nicobar Islands for the naval facilities and the air base on the Island and the pre-feasibility studies for the same has been presented by DCNS France to the Indian Navy. All these developments concur with the IRENA Ocean Energy Technology Brief, June 2014 which favorably considers technical feasibility to build 10MW OTEC plants using current design, manufacturing, deployment techniques and materials, though the actual operating experience is still lacking. Further the review sums up that OTEC has the highest potential when comparing all ocean energy technologies and as many as 98 nations and territories have been identified that have viable OTEC resources in their Exclusive Economic Zones. (EEZ)

Governments in France, Japan, Philippines and South Korea have developed road maps for OTEC development. Indonesia is mapping its OTEC resources. Malaysia is proposing a new law on OTEC and Philippines has been considering feed-in tariffs for OTEC. While delivering the acceptance speech on receiving the 2012 Distinguished Peace Leadership Award from Nuclear Age Peace Foundation, Honorable Tony A de Brum, has informed that Marshall Islands, in partnership with Palau and Micronesia has undertaken studies for establishing OTEC plants and hoped that OTEC will turn these islands from oil dependent basket case economies into net exporter of renewable energy.

OTEC Research in India

National Institute of Ocean Technology (NIOT), Chennai has been engaged in the development of OTEC Technology. A one MW floating OTEC plant was built by NIOT and demonstration trials were conducted off Tuticorin Port. Based on the demonstrations, though a commercial OTEC power plant is yet to be installed in India, LTTD (Low temperature thermal desalination), a technology based on OTEC has been successfully commercialized with land based desalination plants established at Lakshadweep Islands and is operational.

The author and his team of scientists of NIOT had prepared a project report titled "Pre-feasibility studies for commercialization of OTEC power in India" comprising of OTEC resource potential of India and a road map for OTEC power production in India and the same was submitted to National Thermal Power Corporation(NTPC), a power producer in India who sponsored the project in 2004. Considering the OTEC potential of India, being in the tropical region and with a coastline of 7500 km., it is estimated that the OTEC resources could be about 3 Lakh MW of installed capacity in the Indian EEZ (Fig.2). As Ministry of Earth Sciences of India has been on the survey of our EEZ which is ongoing and may result in our EEZ expanding to about 3 million Sq. KMs. from the current 2 million Sq.kms which will further add to our OTEC and Gas Hydrate resources. It is expected that next to wind and solar energy, this energy technology would take off sooner in India and could become the major source of energy for our future generations.

OTEC Cost Estimates

Though OTEC is capital intensive, the zero fuel cost and eco-friendly nature will offset the same in the long run. Also as experience with this technology is still limited with only smaller size plants the cost economics could not be compared readily with other matured renewable energy technologies like wind, solar etc. The capital cost reduces with the larger size plant, and the higher temperature differential. The following cost estimates have been suggested for OTEC plant-ships of various sizes designed for a differential of 220C:

50-60 MW(e) = $ 6000 / KW(e)

60-75 MW(e) = $5000 / KW(e)

75-100MW(e) = $4000 / KW(e).

Further the above cost estimates are empirical and needs to be added with additional costs for site specific conditions and other factors like geographical location of plant, proximity to shore and additional facilities for utility of by-products etc. Specific cost estimates for larger OTEC plants are also available.

A 75 MW OTEC commercial floating plant to be located 10-15 km off from the coast producing 600 MM KWH of electricity annually at $ 0.15/KWH has been estimated at US $ 600 MM and reported in OTC paper 19979 (May 2009). OTEC International LLC an Abell Foundation company, has designs approved in principle by ABS with 25-100 MW capacities and are SPAR based designs. Also innovative design approaches are being evolved by scientists working on OTEC along with offshore engineering professionals. One of the approaches proposed by the author during his tenure with NIOT was to circulate the working fluid in a closed cycle OTEC plant to a condenser located closer to seabed thereby avoiding the pumping of cold sea water to the surface from deep ocean thereby saving considerable cost of the OTEC plant. A patented design with similar concept indicates a cost reduction of 35-45 percent thereby improving the economics of OTEC.

OTEC Economics

The author's paper titled "OTEC Economics -The Perception & the Future" presented in an International conference in 2004 discussed the importance of OTEC for India, being a well placed tropical country. An interesting comparison made between a marginal oil field producing 10000 BOPD for 10 years with a 100MW OTEC plant to be located in the East coast of India at 2004 prices (oil price 25 \$/BBL) revealed that OTEC could be commercially comparable pending few technological challenges on OTEC systems of larger sizes of this order. Over the years and as of now new technological developments in offshore industry show increased confidence levels for building larger OTEC plants towards OTEC commercialization.

A New Approach to OTEC Commercialisation

A new strategy/thinking to the OTEC development cycle Vs Oil price phenomena emerges as of now to even seriously consider and progress rapidly on OTEC commercialization. It appears to be the right time to fulfill the long cherished dreams of OTEC proponents to quickly put up OTEC platforms on a commercial basis. Due to lower oil prices many of the ready to develop deep water oil field projects are being shelved. Further many deep water rigs and FPSOs are going to be idle leading to a crash in prices, thus a potential candidate could be available for combining OTEC facilities onto this platform. Further it is to be noted that deep water fields with water depth more than 1000m which are unviable independently could be combined with OTEC concurrently in modular basis or subsequently with topside replacements and modifications so that the costly investments of the offshore structures are returned economically over long periods as OTEC resource has unlimited life as long as the equipments are operational. By rough estimates it could be possible to share about 40% cost between OTEC and oil production with the same floating plant-ship. This new thinking (that OTEC could be a savior for marginal deep water oil fields) against earlier approach of comparison of OTEC with other energy sources is important considering the fact that consumption of fossil fuels is to be curtailed progressively and OTEC is a base load power(24x7) and energy transfer from OTEC plants could be by subsea cables to shore or even OTEC power could produce hydrogen based fuels, which could be transported to shore for use in transport sector as well, thereby moving towards a non-fossil fuel era, whether before depletion of all fossil fuels or after depletion. Similar approach of combining OTEC with Gas Hydrate production and deep sea mining (Grazing OTEC) would go a long way in establishing OTEC and other renewable sources, all from the sun, as the ultimate future energy source for mankind. As the equatorial zone is like an oil field (OTEC) with an unlimited production capacity India gains to derive the maximum benefit through OTEC power towards energy security.

Principle of Ocean Thermal Energy Conversion (OTEC)

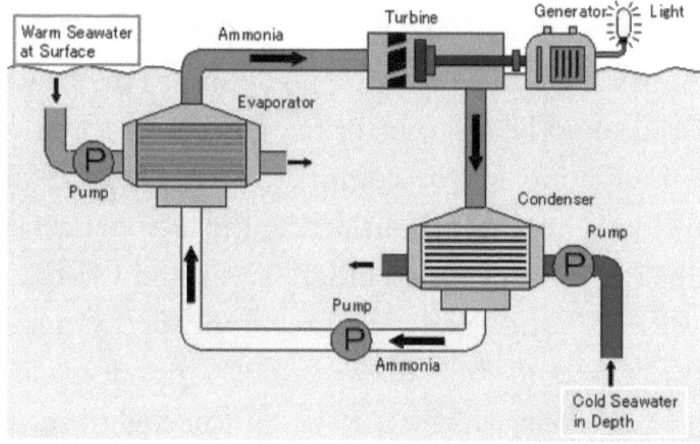

Fig. 1 The Principle of Ocean Thermal Energy Conversion

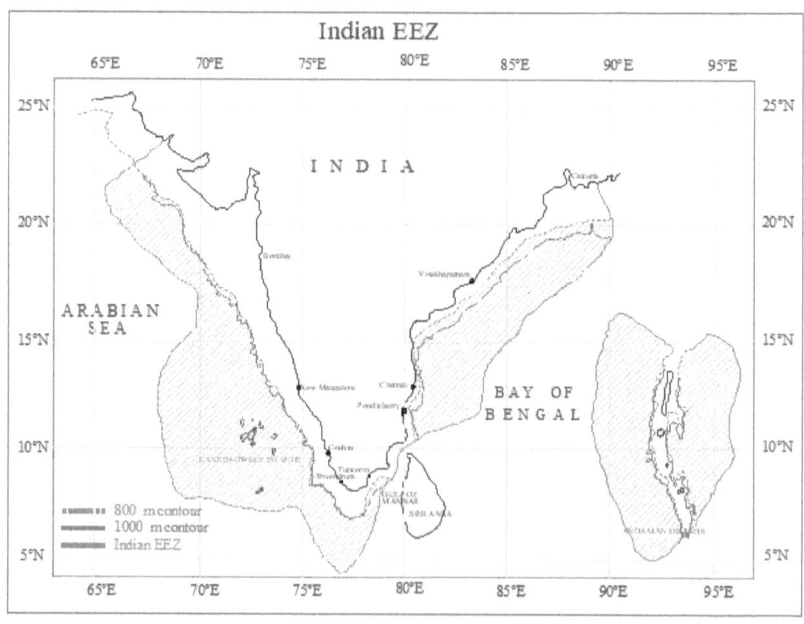

Fig. 2 The OTEC Potential in India

Coastal length	= 7500 km
EEZ area	= 17,05,815 km2
Potential OTEC power	= 3,20,000 MW

References

1. Luis A.Vega, Encyclopedia of sustainability Science & Technology, Springer, Aug 2012 PP 7296-7328.
2. IRENA Ocean Energy Technology Brief, June 2014.
3. T.J. Plock, M. Laboy & J.A. Marti, Ocean Thermal Energy conversion, Technical viability, cost projections and development strategies, OTC conference paper OTC 19979, May 2009.
4. European Patent EP 2395241A2 dt. 14.12.2011 bulletin 2011/50
5. P. Manivannan, L.Sheela Nair and M. Ravindran, OTEC Economics -The Perception and the future, First International conference on Renewable Energy 6-8 Oct 2004, New Delhi.
6. Ocean Thermal Energy Conversion Development Update -A presentation to the World Bank Dec 2013 by OTEC International LLC.
7. Luis A.Vega, OTEC overview in OTEC NEWS.

Extract from PFR, NTPC report

FEASIBILITY STUDY FOR SETTING UP OCEAN THERMAL ENERGY CONVERSION (OTEC) BASED POWER PROJECTS IN INDIA

Sponsor

National Thermal Power Corporation Limited
Noida, New Delhi

Prepared by
Ocean Thermal Energy Conversion Group
NATIONAL INSTITUTE OF OCEAN TECHNOLOGY
(Department of Ocean Development)
Government of India

April 2005

The Project Team

Dr. S. Kathiroli

Director

Team Members

P. Manivannan	L. Sheela Nair
D. Soundarajan	N. Vedhachalam
Dr. Purnima Jalihal	M. Tulsiram
Raju Abraham	R. Sridharan
S. Narayanan	A. Karthikeyan
M. Palaniappan	S. Gowri
S. Muthukumaravel	L. Arokia Prabhu

FOREWORD

Renewable energy was the only source of energy available for mankind till the past few hundred years ever since the discovery of fossil fuels. Though unfortunately we call the renewable energy used by man since thousands of years as non-conventional energy and call the non-renewable fossil fuels as conventional energy which is a misnomer, our endeavor should be to return back to the happy era of renewable energy and call them rightly as conventional energy.

National Thermal Power Corporation (NTPC) a premier power producer in India has rightly taken steps to diversify into renewable energy and approached National Institute of Ocean Technology (NIOT) for preparation of a pre-feasibility study report on commercialization of Ocean Thermal Energy Conversion (OTEC) Power in India, realizing the vast potential of ocean thermal resources of India being in the tropical region and with a coast line of 7500 kms and Exclusive Economic Zone(EEZ) of about 2 million sq.kms which is likely to go up further to 3 million sq.kms after a complete survey of EEZ which has been taken up on priority by Department of Ocean Development (DOD), Govt. of India.

This pre-feasibility study report incorporates the current technology status of OTEC, assessment of OTEC resources in India (East coast, West coast, Andaman & Nicobar Islands, Lakshadweep Islands) and identify the potential for installation of OTEC plants with transmissible power to the main land, pre-feasibility analysis of site specific OTEC plants and recommends a strategy for NTPC to proceed with the commercialization of OTEC power in India.

The co-operation and guidance rendered by Shri O.P. Kalia, General Manager, NTPC, Shri S.G. Gupta, DGM, NTPC and Shri S.P. Thakur, Addl. General Manager, NTPC in the preparation of this report is gratefully acknowledged. Our sincere thanks are also due to Prof. M. Ravindran, Founder Director of NIOT who ventured into the mission of developing OTEC technology in India which is one of the promising future renewable energy resources of the mankind.

(D. Soundararajan)
Group Head-OTEC
Chennai
April 2005

EXECUTIVE SUMMARY

1. Ocean Thermal Energy Conversion (OTEC) is a promising source of renewable energy which can be installed in larger capacities than any other renewable source of energy.

2. Even though OTEC research had started as early as 1970, commercialization of OTEC had not taken place due to less interest shown by developed countries as fossil fuels are available at competitive prices and OTEC research advanced whenever oil prices soared. Another reason for the slow progress of OTEC technology is that best potential for OTEC resources are available with small island communities and developing countries whose funding capacity for research is limited.

3. With the Indian 1 MW OTEC demonstration plant on floating barge is in the final stage, a high level of expertise and confidence exist with National Institute of Ocean Technology (NIOT) towards commercialization of OTEC in India.

4. Though originally, theoretical estimates were made by Indian researchers in IIT Madras that OTEC potential resources in the EEZ of India could be 1,80,000 MW, a re-assessment has been made and presented. The potential OTEC resources could be about 3,24,000 MW of capacity in the Indian EEZ. The installed capacity with transmissible power to the main land with the present day technology is estimated at 55,000 MW. The maximum potential is available in the east coast of India.

5. Site specific feasibility studies and techno-commercial analysis was carried out for three locations and presented. The estimates are based on certain assumptions and extrapolations.

Preliminary estimates and analysis reveal that OTEC with desalination is commercially viable with incentives / support from Govt.

6. It is recommended that the 1st pre-commercial OTEC plant be land based at Kavaratti Island with a capacity of 1.5 MW in one module. The estimated capital expenditure would be approximately Rs. 58 Crores.

7. Upon successful operation of the 1st plant for one year it is recommended to go for a larger floating plant of 40 MW capacity or higher.

Baseline Design / Operating conditions of OTEC plant

	Parameters	Equipment	
1.	Gross power, kW		1000
2.	Temperature, °C	Warm water in	29
3.		Cold water in	7
	Cold water intake, m		1000
4.	CWP dia.(OD),mm	HDPE	1000
5.	Area , m²	Evaporator	3720
		Condenser	3440
6.	Flow rate , kg/s	Warm Water	2100
		Cold Water	1490
7.	Ammonia Flow, kg/s		31.6
8.	Temperature, °C	Warm Water exit	24.6
		Cold Water exit	13.0
9.	Phase change ,°C	Evaporator	23.85
		Condenser	14.14
10	Hydraulic loss, m	Warm water side	5.64
		Cold water side	12.78
11.	Temperature, °C	TG inlet	23.85
		TG outlet	14.14
12.	Pressure, bar abs	TG inlet	9.70
		TG outlet	7.09
13.	Pumping power, kW	Warm Water	145
		Cold Water	233
14.	Net power, kW		605

Floating barge with OTEC plant

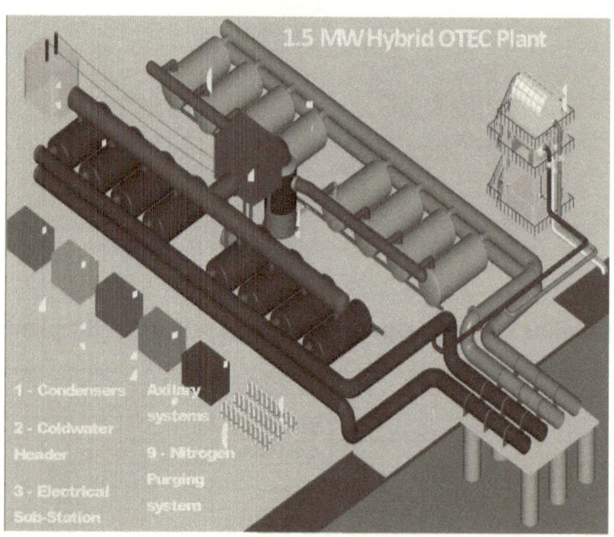

1 - Condensers	8 - Desalination plant Auxiliary
2 - Coldwater Header	systems
3 - Electrical Sub-Station	9 - Nitrogen Purging system
4 - Turbine room	10 - Centralised cooling system
5 - Separator	11 - Compressed Air system
6 - Evaporators	12 - DG Set room
7 - Warmwater Header	13 - Safety System
	14 - Chlorine dosing system

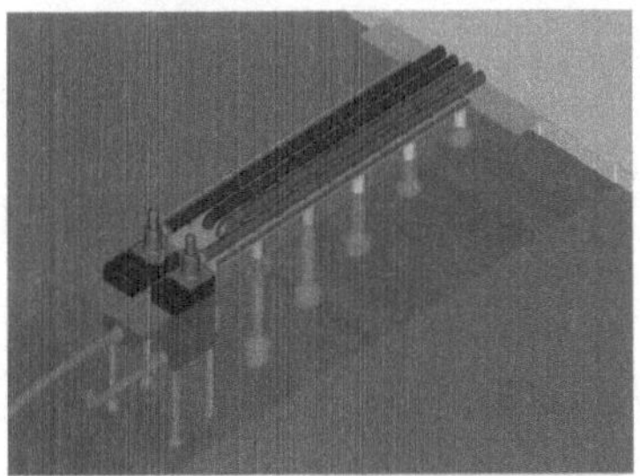

The trestle for sea water intake point

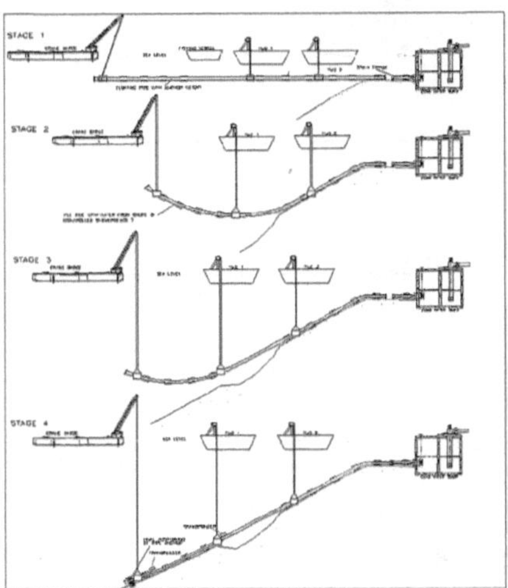

Deployment scheme for cold water pipe for Kavaratti

TABLE -36
Comparison of Cost for the Proposed OTEC plants in India

N o	Plant Location	Capacity of the plant (MW net)	Capital Cost (Rs. Crores)		O & M Cost (Crores/year)	Revenue (Crores/year)		Total Revenue (Crores/year)	IRR (%)	Cost of power generated (Rs/ kWh)	Remarks
			OTEC	Desalination		Power	Water				
1	Small Islands (Kavaratti)	a. 1.5 MW	55	3	2.22	4.5	2.10	6.60	5	9.85	100% Capex
									7	7.63	80% Capex
		b.2.5 x 2 = 5 MW	105	3	3.58	17.64	2.10	19.74	15	3.33	100% Capex
									20	2.13	80% Capex
2	Large Islands (Andaman Islands)	a. 4 x 10 MW with desalination	722	90	26.80	141.3	42.0	183.3	18	3.91	100% Capex
									23	2.78	80% Capex
		b. 4 x 10 MW without desalination	696	——	25.00	141.3	—	141.3	17	4.82	
									22	3.85	100% Capex 80% Capex
3	Main Land India (Cheyyur)	a. 4 x 10 MW with desalination	742	180	28.3	82.25	84.0	166.25	15	2.96	100% Capex
									20	1.69	80% Capex
		b. 4 x 10 MW without desalination	702	——	25.2	82.25	—	82.25	6	4.86	
									9	3.89	100% Capex 80% Capex

Note:
1. Only 6 lakh litres of fresh water production per day is considered for Kavaratti which is 1/6th of the feasible generation capacity of a 1.5 MW plant. For A&N 120 lakhs per day is considered against a feasible capacity of the 480 lakhs per day capacity.
2. The power factor is considered only 0.6 for Kavaratti out of the possible value of 0.8 for an OTEC plant. All other locations the pf is considered as 0.7 conservatively.
3. The cost of power at Kavaratti and Andaman is considered as 6 Rs/Unit for revenue calculation and the cost of fresh water as 10 Paise per litre. At Cheyyur the cost of power is taken as 3.5 Rs/ Unit and the fresh water cost is 5 Paise per litre.
4. The cost of power is estimated considering 4% deprecation, 10% interest, and 3% O&M of the capital cost. The revenue from air-conditioning or aqua-culture is not accounted in the calculation of power cost.

THE ROAD MAP AHEAD

Submission of pre-feasibility report and recommendation to NTPC management

After review and acceptance of pre-feasibility report of NIOT it is suggested that the first pre-commercial plant may be approved for implementation by NTPC management in principle for working out a detailed project report including geophysical and geotechnical surveys and EIA studies. NIOT is fully equipped to carry out the surveys and EIA studies.

Detailed project report

Based on the decision by the management, Detailed Project Report (DPR) for a single unit of 1.5 MW net OTEC plant could be worked out. For better application of the latest technologies available in the OTEC field and offshore industries, NTPC may select a reputed engineering company for the detailed engineering of the OTEC plant and offshore facilities. NIOT will assist as a consultant in the review and finalisation of the detailed project report or this DPR could be prepared jointly by NTPC & NIOT. As recommended in the pre-feasibility study, a hybrid cycle OTEC plant with desalinated water production up to 600 m3 per day is commercially viable with incentives / support from Govt. for implementation at Kavaratti.

Incentives from Govt.

As notified by the Govt. of India, Ministry of Finance, Department of Economic Affairs (Infrastructure section), under the guidelines on support to Public Private Partnerships in Infrastructure issued during August 2004, funding is available for infrastructure schemes under power and water supply. As per these guidelines viability gap funding upto 20% of the project cost is available. As OTEC power is renewable and environmental friendly, if a joint venture partner is identified by NTPC under the scheme, the project could be made commercially very attractive. If further incentives like tax-holidays and subsidies for generation of renewable and eco-friendly power is available the economics would improve further. Looking at the web site various commercial organizations in the international market are willing to invest on OTEC partially with an understanding for further deployment of OTEC power plants. It is submitted that a tie up could be made with one of the reputed organizations and a joint venture project could be established for the proposed first pre-commercial OTEC plant.

Implementation of the OTEC plant

The project could be split into onshore part and offshore part and could be implemented under two contracts or it could be implemented as a single turnkey project. The total duration of the turnkey project is expected to be around 24 months. Tender document for the works could be made through the engineering consultant who is engaged for the detailed project report and implemented.

Shri. MRN. Swamy's collection/compilation on retirement day.

THANK YOU MR. MANIVANNAN
- AN ONGCIAN OF RARE INTELLIGENCE
AND EXCEPTIONAL INTEGRITY

Mr. P Manivannan, DGM (Mech) is retiring from the services of ONGC on 31 March 2017 at RTI, Chennai. He possesses the rare virtues of simplicity and an attitude of doing nothing but WORK, WORK and WORK alone. Except for a handful who know him intimately, Mr. Manivannan is neither well known among ONGCians, nor half as popular as a man of his worth should be.

Though Mr. Manivannan's works have spoken for itself and has benefitted ONGC, a listing of his salient achievements serve as a tribute to his lifelong services. The following list of his accomplishments are only indicative and not exhaustive, to sustain the readers' interest.

Mr. P.Manivannan joined ONGC in 1982 as a GT (M.Tech from IIT Chennai). He was groomed in field of offshore Engineering and Technologies. He was ably trained by stalwarts in the field who were known as task masters. To name a few- Mr. K. Anjaneyan, Dr. B. K Bhattacharya, Dr. Hariharan (EIL), Mr. C.K.Srinivasan, Mr. M.N.Madhava, Mr. E Venugopal and Mr. M.Thyagaraj.

He contributed to around 10 offshore platform projects and 2 onshore terminals. These included the Heera Field from scratch and a few other well platform projects in the west coast and Ravva field, GS-15/23 development and PY-3 field development with technical support to JV group etc. in East coast (ie, more than 10 offshore projects including onshore terminals).

His paper "Reduction in Mudmat weight of offshore platforms by a new construction technique" attracted appreciations from ONGC C&MD Mr. S.K.Manglik. The paper was published in ISOPE-91 which can be accessed even now through Google.

He was instrumental in forming a team of in-house talented engineers in offshore engineering services to design, review and fabricate/install, supervise, initially with a backup consultant, to economise on the need of consultancy services.

Mr. Manivannan was awarded "Professional of the year" in 1999 for the project GS-15/23 in east coast.

He was a trouble shooter for all offshore engineering problems, he was successful in attending to the complaint that Gs-15/23 platforms are unusable and the rig Sagar Ratna docked at Gs-23-1 could not re-enter the well due to alignment problems, the well guides are not proper was the complaint.

While at Jorhat (2005-2008), he played a significant role in reviving the Trunk pipeline project between Borolla and Khoraghat by preparing detailed techno-commercial feasibility report justifying the 65 Km trunk pipeline. Considering the local conditions in Assam, the tendering was done from Mumbai and he successfully implemented the same.

His experience in Project Management came in handy to put back the housing project in Anna Nagar, Chennai on a right course. As Head Maintenance, he organized inking of an MOU with Tamil Nadu Housing Board and all the design activities were completed, sanction obtained and spade work done for tendering.

He was requested by NIOT for his deputation to work as Mission Head for World's First 1 MW Ocean Thermal Energy Conversion (OTEC) Project, a Jai Vigyan Project of Government of India under the Ministry of Earth Sciences (MoES).

It is not the absence of opportunities which made Mr. Manivannan to continue in ONGC. Inspite of the best-in-class credentials in the field, it was his whole-hearted commitment to the National Energy Security that made him to continue and retire from ONGC, notwithstanding a slow growth. But Mr. Manivannan is satisfied as many of his Mentees have grown into responsible positions in this energy major. This makes me to remember an adage "Do not worry if you are not successful as successful people Enrich themselves from the society, than Enriching the society."

Thank you Mr. Mani for Enriching ONGC and the society.

MRN Swamy
Chief Manager (MM)

SRINIVASA RAO AVALASOMAYAJULA, CAMBAY
Deputy General Manager (HR)
March 28, 2017
Dear Sir,

I, at the outset would like to thank the editors of or.net for publishing such an article. It really shows that we as an organization value and cherish the contributions of our fellow ongcians! I would also like to thank my good friend Swamy for highlighting the achievements of one of the silent workers of our organization, the unsung soldier who toils away without expecting any reward or award! It has been my good fortune of knowing Sh. Manivannan from his days in Jorhat and also till my transfer to Cambay earler this year. He is truly a gentle gentleman and a pleasure to work with, in fact as the liasion officer for the OBC and OBC Association he was very much instrumental in maintaining the rosters in Chennai in the required manner. He was also a member in many of our recruitment boards and was very keen and interested in selection of the right candidates for the ONGC. It will be a big loss to the organization, but on the personal front a great future lies ahead of him, as already he has some consultancy and research assignments in his pocket! Wishing him good health and success in his future assignments!

RONADA MATH KOTRESH, KAKINADA

General Manager (Civil)

March 25, 2017

I worked closely with him in E&C div in Mumbai during 1983 to 1991 and his indepth knowledge on concept development of Heera field development first platforms HA, HRA and HB and development was implemented in I st phase will go into history of ONGC. His contribution in Phase II development of Heera field from concept stage to commissioning will be remebered for ever. Whatever knowledge gathered during my initial stages of my career is due to my close association with Mr. Manivannan during execution of aforesaid Heera project implementation

I was closely associated as co author in his technical paper "Reduction in Mudmat weight of offshore platforms by a new construction technique" attracted appreciations from ONGC, C & MD Mr. SK Manglik. The paper was published in ISOPE-91. His innovative idea was brought into international paper and subsequently this technique was patented in India in 1991.

Thanks Mr. Swamy for your efforts in highlighting Mr. Manivannan's achivements in development of two virgin fields, Heera in Western offshore and GS 15/23 field in Eastern offshore. He is real energy soldier of Indian offshore fields.

I wish him Happy, Healthy and Active superannuated life.

RM KOTRESH
Project Manager KG-DWN-98/2 proj
EOA Kakinada

N SUJANI, Chennai
Senior HR Executive
March 24, 2017
ALL THE VERY BEST SIR

GOUR MOHAN DASS, Ahmedabad
Deputy General Manager (Chemistry)
March 24, 2017
Hats off to Mr. Manivannan Sir!! Best wishes sir.
Effort of Mr. MRN Swamy is really worth appreciating for
enlightening us about the superb technocrat and wonderful
human being that Mani Sir is.
Many thanks and best wishes.

GOPALA KRISHNA RAVI, AGARTALA
Chief Manager (Materials Management)
March 24, 2017
Dear Swamy, so nice of you bringing to limelight an unsung hero.
Best wishes to Mani Sir.

PURABI DUTTA CHOWDHURY, Delhi
Deputy General Manger (Production)
March 24, 2017
Thanks for introducing us to this unsung hero. My salute to this
great soul. Feel proud to be a fellow ongcian. Regards and best
wishes to Shri Mani Sir.

SUBASH CHAND, IPC/GEOPIC/ONGC ACADEMY

Superintending Geophysicist (Surface)

March 23, 2017

All the best Sir

KISHORE KUMAR, DEHRADUN

Superintending Engineer (Production)

March 23, 2017

All the best Sir

K. MANIVANNAN, ANKLESHWAR

Deputy General Manager (Materials Management)

March 23, 2017

All the best to Manivannan sir

K. KANTHAPPAN, DELHI

Deputy General Manager (Finance & Accounts)

March 23, 2017

Thanks Mr. Swamy for writing this excellent and apt article which is a tribute to Shri Manivannan-one of the unsung heros of ONGC.

I had close official association with him when he was working in E&C, Chennai under great leader Mr. CK Srinivasan. My friendship with him continues.

To quote one instance - while Ravva Platform Installation and hook up work was going on, at once stage they had a problem of hooking up the Coflexiup pipe through the J tube. The team was stuck and work was getting delayed. There was pressure from the management and Minisitry to start production. Mr. Manivannan came up with the idea of putting I tube in the Platform to hook up the pipeline. Then the work was done & production started much to the relief of top management of ONGC and Ministry. (I am not a technical person and any techncial error in this message may be pardoned). This was narrated by Mr. CK Srinivasan, the then GGM(Technical) and Head of E&C Division, Chennai, in his retirement farewell speech.

The real tribute was Mr. CK in his retirement farewell speech had stated like this "if at all I want to give credit to anyone for the successful completion of Ravva Platfrom & Pipeline installation and commissioning work, it is only to Mr. P Manivannan". It is like getting Brammha Rishi Title from Vasistha."

Apart from this technical capabilities, he is very good contract manager also. I had personal experience of this when we as a team worked for the Arbitration case of M/s Hindustan Shipyard Ltd & its sub-contractor M/s ESSAR OFFSHORE for the same Ravva installation contract.

I am reminded of one Tamil Cinema song by great poet Kannadasan - "All the talented people do not succeed and all those succeeded are not talented."

We all know that Mr. Manivannan is a contended man he will live happily.

I wish him a happy, healthy and peaceful retired life.

GULLAPALLI KOTESWARA RAO, CHENNAI
Chief Manager (HR)
March 23, 2017
All the best to Mr. Manivannan Sir

R. PANDIARAJ, Karaikal
Deputy General Manager (Electrical)
March 22, 2017

Very well described about the Achievements of Mr. Manivannan. Unfortunately in ONGC, maintenanance engineers are neither recognized nor get their due elevation. Of course, ONGC is not for core engineering disciplines. So, there is no surprise that he didn't get his elevation even after 10 years at his current position.

Let us wish him a Happy and healthy retired life.

மீண்டும் அடிமையாக

மீனாவின் முகத்தில் கடுகைப் போட்டால் "டப் டப்பென்று" வெடித்து விடும், அத்தனைக் கோபமாகப் புலம்பிக் கொண்டிருந்தாள்.

"மாதம் சுளையாக ஐம்பதாயிரம் சம்பளம் வருவதை யாராவது வேண்டாம் என்பார்களா? என் கணவர் சொல்கிறாரே… இவர் வாங்குகிற 15,000/- சம்பளத்தில் வருமானவரி, பிடிப்புகள் போக கைக்கு வருவது ஏழாயிரமோ, எட்டாயிரமோ! இதில், பெருமைவாய்ந்த சென்னை மாநகரத்தில் பாதிசம்பளத்தை வீட்டு வாடகையாகக் கொடுத்துவிட்டு உன்னைப்பிடி, என்னைப்பிடி என்று துரத்திப்பிடிக்கிற வாழ்க்கை நடத்தும் நடுத்தரவர்க்கத்து இன்ஞினியர் சாருக்கு மாதம் 50,000/- தரும் கம்பெனி கசக்கிறதா என்ன? கம்பெனிக்கார அதிகாரிகள் பளபளவென்கிற சீலோ காரில் வீடு தேடிவந்து தங்கள் கம்பெனியில் முக்கியப் பதவியில் வந்து சேர்ந்துவிடும்படி வெற்றிலைப்பாக்கு வைக்காத குறையாய் அழைத்துவிட்டுச் செல்கிறார்கள். எதற்கும் அசைந்து கொடுக்க மாட்டேன்கிறாரே இந்த மனிதர்"

"அம்மா, இந்த வருடம் ஸ்கூல் யூனிஃபார்ம் கலர் மாத்திட்டாங்க, புதுசா ரெண்டு செட் வாங்கனும். அப்பாக்கிட்ட ஆயிரம் ரூபா வாங்கிவை ஒ.கே? சுலபமாக சொல்லிவிட்டு கிரிக்கெட் மட்டையுடன் பறக்கிறான். +1 படிக்கும் பெரிய மகன். இவனுக்கு டியூஷன் பீஸே மாதம் 500 ரூபாய் ஆகிறது. ஆயிரம் பெருமூச்சு சீறிவருகிறது. மீனாவிடமிருந்து.

"அம்மா…" என்று கண்ணைக் கசக்கியப்படி வந்து நின்ற மகளுடன் இரண்டு மூன்று பெண் குழந்தைகள் துணைக்கு. "என்னடி… ஆச்சு… ஏன் அழறே? பெற்ற வயிறு சங்கடத்தில் பதற மற்ற பெண்கள் முகத்தைத் தாழ்த்தி சிரிக்கின்றன.

"ஓஹோ… அதானா விஷயம்! அடிப்பெண்ணே எட்டாம் வகுப்பிலேயே உட்கார்ந்துட்டியா? சரிசரி, பாத்ரூமுக்குப் போ வரேன்" என்று சொல்லி தோழிகளுக்கு இனிப்புக் கொடுத்தனுப்பிவிட்டு.. பெண்ணைக் குளிப்பாட்டுகையில் மனதில் பாரம் ஏறிக்கொள்கிறது மீனாவுக்கு. "இவளுக்கென்று நல்லதாக நாலு டிரெஸ் எடுக்க, கழுத்துக்கும் காதுக்கும் மெலிதாக நகை செய்ய, பணத்துக்கு எங்கே போவது? பெரியவனை அடுத்தவருடம் ஒரு நல்ல கோர்ஸில் சேர்க்க… எல்லாவற்றுக்கும் பணம் வேண்டுமே.

இந்த மனிதருக்கு ஏன் புரியமாட்டேன்கிறது? இன்றைக்கு இரண்டில் ஒன்று கேட்டுவிட வேண்டியதுதான்.

ராகவன் வேலையிலிருந்து திரும்பியவுடன் கேட்கிறாள் மீனா. என்னங்க, நம்ம பொண்ணு பெரியவளாயிட்டா. பையனுக்கும் புது யூனிஃபார்ம் வாங்கணும். இனி போகப் போக அவன் படிப்பு செலவுக்கும் பணம் தேவைதானே. இந்த அரசாங்க உத்யோகத்தில் நாற்காலியைத் தேய்த்துக்கொண்டு இளித்தவாய்த்தனமாய் எல்லா வேலைகளையும் உங்க தலையிலேயே போட்டுக்கிட்டு, மேலதிகாரிகள் செய்யும் லஞ்சலாவண்யங்களைக் காணப் பொறுக்காமல் வயிற்றில் அல்சரும், அசிடிட்டியும் வளர்த்துக் கொண்டு, வருகிற வருமானத்தில் வரியைக் கட்டிவிட்டு மீதி கொண்டு வருகிற பணத்தில் எப்படி இந்த செலவுகளையெல்லாம் சமாளிக்க முடியும்? ஏன் பேசாம இருக்கீங்க? அவங்களும் ஒரு மாசமா உங்களை பல வழிகள்ல கேட்டுப் பாக்கராங்க, நீங்க நல்லா வேலை தெரிஞ்சவர்னுதானே, உங்களை அவங்க கம்பெனியில சேர்த்துக்க ஆசைப்படராங்க. கைநிறைய சம்பளம், கார், வீடுன்னு எல்லா வசதியும் கிடைக்கக் கூடிய வேலைய ஏன் வேணாம்னு சொல்றீங்க? வாய் திறந்து பேசுங்க, மீனாவின் உணர்ச்சிமயமான கத்தலுக்கு பதில் வருகிறது, அவரிடமிருந்து.

மீனா.., உன்னுடைய கோபமும், தேவையும் எனக்குப் புரியுது. பற்றாக்குறையிலதான் நம்ம நாடு இப்ப இயங்கிக்கிட்டிருக்கு… அதுக்காக மறுபடியும் போய், ஐயா! வெள்ளைக்கார துரைமாரே வாங்க! எங்களால முடியலை, நீங்களாவது நாட்டைத் தூக்கி நிறுத்துங்கன்னு கெஞ்சமுடியுமா? இதுக்காகவா நம்ம நாட்டின்

சுதந்திரத்திற்காக, தங்கள் உயிரையே தியாகம் பண்ண ஒவ்வொருத்தரும் அணு அணுவா சித்ரவதை அனுபவிச்சாங்க? தங்களோட குடும்பத்தை பெரிசா நினைக்காம ஜெயில்ல இருந்து பலவித துன்பங்களை சகிச்சிக்கிட்டாங்க? இதோ இப்ப என்னை வேலைக்குக் கூப்பிடறவங்களும் வெளிநாட்டு துரைமார்கள் தான். ஏன்னா, நான் அறிவாளி, புத்திசாலி, நல்ல உழைப்பாளி. ஆனால் நான் என் தாய்நாட்டின் சொத்து. என்னுடைய நாடு, நாட்டின் வளர்ச்சி இதுக்காக நான் உழைக்கணுமே தவிர, இந்த மண்ணிலேயே கொஞ்சம் கொஞ்சமா கால்வைத்து நம்ம மக்களின் உழைப்பையும், நம்ம நாட்டோட செல்வத்தையும் அபகரிச்சிகிட்டுப் போக வந்து இறங்கியிருக்காங்களே அந்த வெள்ளைக்கார கம்பெனிக்காக இல்ல, புரிஞ்சுதா?

மீனாவுக்கு புரிந்துவிட்டது என்பது அவள் தன் கணவரின் கைகளைப் பிடித்துக் கொண்டு பெருமையுடன் புன்னகைப்பதிலேயே தெரிகிறது.

எழுதியவர்

ஷீலா மணிவண்ணன்

க/பெ. ப. மணிவண்ணன்

9, 2வது மெயின் ரோடு, ஆபிசர்ஸ் காலனி,

ஆதம்பாக்கம், சென்னை-88

Patriotism

Patriotism is the feeling of love, devotion, and a sense of attachment to one's country. A true patriot not only works towards building his nation but also inspires others to do so. Patriotism is voluntary. It is a feeling of loyalty. It is supporting your country all the time and your Government when it deserves it. Your contribution to your mother land should be greater than what you have consumed from your mother land. Let us salute our Nation.

- V Balakrishnan
DGM, ONGC (Retd)
(In daily quotes)